In Black
and White

C000217557

In Black and White

NATHALIE SEYMOUR

Published by
British Association for Adoption & Fostering
(BAAF)
Saffron House
6–10 Kirby Street
London EC1N 8TS
www.baaf.org.uk

Charity registration 275689

© Nathalie Seymour, 2007

British Library Cataloguing in Publication Data
A catalogue record for this book is available from the
British Library

ISBN 978 1 905664 10 8

Photographs on cover posed by models by istockphoto.com
and John Birdsall Photography
Designed by Andrew Haig & Associates
Typeset by Fravashi Aga, London
Printed in Great Britain by T J International
Trade distribution by Turnaround Publisher Services, Unit 3,
Olympia Trading Estate, Coburg Road, London N22 6TZ

All rights reserved. Apart from any fair dealing for the purposes of
research or private study, or criticism or review, as permitted under
the Copyright, Designs and Patents Act 1988, this publication may
not be reproduced, stored in a retrieval system, or transmitted in
any form or by any means, without the prior written permission of
the publishers.

The moral right of the author has been asserted in accordance with
the Copyright, Designs and Patents Act 1988.

BAAF is the leading UK-wide membership organisation for all
those concerned with adoption, fostering and child care issues.

Acknowledgements

I would like to thank the many friends who have read this book in its various forms over the years. I am grateful to them all for their time, encouragement and comments, which helped the evolution of the book since I began writing it many years ago. My grateful thanks also go to Kay Beaumont, Phillida Sawbridge and Perlita Harris who have read and commented on the most recent draft. I should also like to thank the editor, Hedi Argent, for her careful attention and constructive suggestions, and Felicity Collier and Shaila Shah at BAAF for creating the opportunity for publication. I am indebted to Rita for reading the draft and taking the time to suggest detailed changes. Most of all, my thanks go to Tom for his invaluable contribution to our discussions about the many issues the book tackles and for his support throughout the time of writing.

All the names of the characters in this story have been changed to preserve their anonymity.

About the author

Nathalie Seymour is the pseudonym of a retired civil servant with a background in social work. She has collaborated in a number of published research papers, articles and textbooks.

The Our Story series
This book is part of BAAF's Our Story series, which explores adoption experiences as told by adoptive parents.

Also available in this series: *An Adoption Diary* by Maria James and *Flying Solo* by Julia Wise.

The series editor
Hedi Argent is the editor of this series. She is an independent adoption consultant, trainer and freelance writer. She is the author of *Find me a Family* (Souvenir Press, 1984), *Whatever Happened to Adam?* (BAAF, 1998), *Related by Adoption* (BAAF, 2004), *One of the Family* (BAAF, 2005), *Ten Top Tips for Placing Children in Permanent Families* (BAAF, 2006), the co-author of *Taking Extra Care* (BAAF, 1997), and *Dealing with Disruption* (BAAF, 2006), and the editor of *See you Soon* (BAAF, 1995), *Staying Connected* (BAAF, 2002) and *Models of Adoption Support* (BAAF, 2003). She has also contributed four illustrated booklets to the children's series published by BAAF: *What Happens in Court?* (2003), *What is Contact?* (2004), *What is a Disability?* (2004) and *Life Story Work* (2005) with Shaila Shah.

For Danny and Rita

Contents

Foreword

It has taken thirty years to write this story as it happened. Thirty years of struggle, rewards, challenges, great sadness, and finally hope. Nathalie Seymour and her husband, Tom, wanted to have a family. They knew they couldn't have biological children; adoption was their aim and their wish. At a time when black children drifted in the public care system, it seemed right and desirable to establish a transracial family. Many liberal minded white adopters were doing the same. But Nathalie and Tom went further: they wanted their children to remain connected to their birth family and to grow up with pride in their heritage. Today, "open adoptions" are becoming more usual, but thirty years ago Nathalie and Tom were breaking new ground. Neither they, nor the professionals advising them, foresaw where this would lead and how deeply it would affect the children, their birth family and the whole process of adoption.

Social work is prey to fashion; the three themes of this book – transracial placements, open adoptions and adoption support – have all undergone fundamental changes since the early 70s. Legislation, regulations and guidance have moved the goalposts.

Rita and Danny would not be placed with a white family today. But between 1965 and 1969 the British Adoption Project was highly praised for finding white families to adopt black children, and other organisations quickly followed suit. We had to learn from black adopted children over the next two decades that being brought up by white people, however successful in terms of personal relationships, is a high price to pay in terms of identity and self-esteem. The language began to change as the practice changed. We no longer talk about ethnic minorities: if anyone is in the minority in this multicultural world of ours, it is surely white Europeans. We recognise that some people live in minority ethnic groups in countries other than their own, which is a different thing altogether. But although we all belong to the same race – the human race, whatever our ethnicity, culture or religion – we go on talking about transracial and "same-race" family placements. It clearly takes language longer to catch up.

Most local authorities and voluntary adoption agencies now have "same-race" adoption policies but the criteria are becoming less rigid as our ethnic heritages become more complex. It is very hard to find a family to match a child's ethnicity if her mother is half Bosnian and half Irish and her father is half Iranian and half Nigerian. The best that can be done is to meet as many as possible of a child's whole raft of needs, including their need to maintain and enhance their cultural connections.

The legal process of adoption has been amended to emphasise the paramount interests of the child and the importance of keeping children connected to their birth family. Kinship carers – family and close friends – must be considered before all others when children have to be separated from their birth parents. And contact (previously described as access) has to be part of every Adoption Support Plan, which is now a statutory requirement whenever a child is placed for adoption.

It is very unlikely that the adopters in this book would have to go through as many legal hurdles today as they did, and the contact arrangements with the children's birth family would be agreed before placement, supported by the adoption agency, and regularly reviewed. Danny and Rita and the adopters would not be subjected to the risks and danger they had to endure in their efforts to "keep in touch".

Adoption support, obligatory since the Adoption and Children Act 2002 (England and Wales) covers every stage of adoption (before and after placement, and before and after an Adoption Order is made) until the child reaches the age of 18. Nowadays, Nathalie and Tom would have a right to consistent adoption support and would not be expected to deal with complex and even dangerous contact situations on their own. Adoption support also has to include preparing children for adoption: Danny was not ready when he was placed with the adopters and he was not ready when the judge made the order; Nathalie and Tom were left unsupported with yet another potentially disruptive problem.

This is an unusual story, bravely told as it was. In today's social climate it is not easy to admit smacking your precious adopted daughter, even if you have reached the end of your tether. In spite of all the tribulations and sorrows, Natalie has written a positive story that celebrates the strength of families and relationships.

Hedi Argent
Series Editor
January 2007

1

Meeting Rita

Tom stopped the car outside an end-of-terrace house in a quiet riverside suburb. Every window was net curtained, giving no hint of the life inside, but the front garden with its patch of grass and borders of early summer flowers looked pretty. I glanced at Tom as we approached the door, wondering, but with suddenly no time to ask, whether he felt the mixture of anticipation and nervousness that I was feeling.

When the door opened, I forgot my fears. There was Rita, at 17 months little more than a baby, smiling a welcome. She was a black child. But that single word "black" doesn't do justice to the golden brown of her face, the darker brown of her legs and the ivory of the palm stretched out towards us. She sat on the hip of Sandie Clark, her foster carer, her bare feet dangling. Sandie, blonde curls contrasting with Rita's black ones, ushered us in to meet a circle of faces. Several members of the family, apart from Rita, were appraising us, including Sandie's husband, Toby, and their twelve-year-old adopted son.

Sandie put Rita down and she danced into the centre of the Clark family. The conversation focused on Rita's behaviour and her actions as everyone competed to tell us all about her. Rita was big for her age and strongly built. She was agile and confident and her little face gleamed with fun. She kept her distance from us at first, but she climbed and scrambled over the others with ease, brown eyes sparkling. She drank tea noisily from a bottle as the family recounted anecdotes in which she starred, and described her likes and dislikes. 'If she's quiet for a long time, you know she's up to mischief!' or 'She likes rock music.'

Sandie turned to me, when she had finished serving tea to everyone.

'You know about Rita's mother, I suppose?' she said.

I nodded. Rita's mother, Cynthia, was suffering from a serious mental illness.

'She comes here about once every three months. She stays ten minutes, says almost nothing at all, but just watches the television and then leaves – she keeps a taxi waiting,' said Sandie, her tone making it clear that the visits were unsatisfactory occasions. I thought Cynthia might feel ill at ease, coming into this confident and close-knit family, trying to seem a mother to a child she had in many ways lost.

After a little enticing, Rita came up to play with Tom. When he picked her up, she pulled at his beard and tried to remove his glasses. By the end of the visit, she was sitting on my knee.

Sandie was pleased to see Rita taking notice of us, but she carefully avoided asking us any questions about our intentions. We said goodbye, promising that the social worker who had arranged for us to meet Rita would be in touch.

We had only driven a few yards down the street when I said: 'She's so alive and so loveable!'

Tom was quick to agree. A silence followed. My mind went back to the two years we had spent thinking about and applying to adopt a child. Rita was the first child we had met as a result. I looked across at Tom as we headed home and we both started talking together. We wanted her to come and live with us.

Rita had captivated us. We felt a groundless confidence that we could deal with the difficulties of her circumstances, but we wondered how we could compensate for her rich experience in her large and warm-hearted foster family. The next day, sure of our decision even in the cooler light of the morning, we rang Sarah, our social worker, and began to discuss plans for Rita's move into our home. We would spend a month preparing her as she would need time to get to know us. We arranged to visit her twice a week and bring her home for the day on the last two Saturdays – on the second she would stay overnight with us.

When we returned to see the Clarks, Sandie was delighted at our decision and welcomed us in. I gave her a photograph to use in helping Rita to talk about us and we watched Rita playing as we discussed her future.

'She will be upset for a while, but she'll get used to you. She might even go off her food for a week or two, although I'd be surprised, because she has a good appetite!' Sandie said, laughing as we all looked at Rita's plump little frame.

Sandie was a highly experienced foster carer of babies and toddlers. She explained that there never had been any question of Rita remaining with the Clarks, even though she had lived with them since she was four months old. Despite her matter-of-fact manner, we knew that Sandie and her family would miss Rita.

'Well, I'll just get Rita's coat and you can take her out for a walk,' she said.

Taking Rita out was an act of significance and gave us our first responsibility towards her. She accompanied us without protest, plodding ahead, refusing to hold hands or to sit in her pushchair. As we were passing a blackened old brick wall, she stopped, pointed a finger and said decisively, 'Dirty'. When we were bowling home with Rita in the pushchair, she set up a chant of 'Mummy, Mummy,

Mummy'.

'She's keen to get back to Sandie,' I said.

'No, she's just telling us about Sandie,' said Tom. It was the first of many conversations about what Rita was thinking.

Indoors, Rita's sombreness vanished and she jumped around us, chuckling and gleeful, as if she were sharing a joke or telling us she was not always distant. She was obviously relieved to be home again.

The month of introductions passed quickly. We became used to taking Rita for walks to the river nearby. She learned to recognise us and we felt she enjoyed our visits. The time soon came for her first visit to us. When we arrived home, Rita dashed in and ran around the house exploring. She played with some of the toys we had bought or been given for her, and Tom played the piano and sang nursery rhymes. This went down well and we started to relax. We took Rita home in the late afternoon, singing songs to make her laugh, which she did readily.

When it was time for Rita to stay overnight with us, we put her cot by our bed and let her stay up as long as she wanted to, just as Sandie did. She stayed up brightly until eleven o'clock in the evening and we crawled exhausted to bed not long afterwards. The following morning, we took Rita back to the Clarks for her last night with them and spent our last day together as a couple without children.

In spite of the preparations, we felt a mixture of emotions. We were on the brink of an enormous change in our lives. Neither of us had much experience of children. We had spent time thinking about a family and discussing how we could have one, but we had no real idea of what we were doing. To have a child in the usual way would have been change enough, but to intervene in the life of a child who was totally unconnected with us seemed extraordinary. We were chastened by the weight of our decision and yet excited by the prospect of life with Rita.

Tom and I grew up in ordinary suburbs at opposite ends of London in the 1950s. We were in our mid-twenties when we met as social workers. Tom specialised in helping people who had mental health problems. He was passionate about music and played blues, jazz, rock and classical music on piano and guitar. He liked sport and played tennis. He was kind and good-natured. I worked with children. I was also keen to travel and see the world. I knew before I met Tom that I would not be able to have children.

In our early thirties, we started to think about a family. For us this meant adoption. We knew that we would have to submit to a long application process and that few babies were available. In 1977, we started applying to adoption agencies and, after initial contact with several, we narrowed the choice down to our own local authority, where the adoption unit had a good reputation and we would not have to wait too long to be assessed. A social worker, Jackie, interviewed us over a number of months and in addition we attended group discussions at the adoption unit with other aspiring adoptive parents.

The assessment process focused on our suitability as parents of children past infancy, helping us to crystallise our ideas. We wanted a child as young as possible. We also decided that we could offer a home to a child with mild disabilities, but we did not feel confident enough to parent a severely physically disabled child or one with learning difficulties.

We wanted a child from any ethnic background. Transracial adoption was acceptable within the white community in late 1970s Britain and was well regarded. Research using psychological and educational measures showed that such children were as well adjusted as other adopted children, but their ethnic and/or cultural dislocation were not examined in these studies and remain contentious. We took the view, which would perhaps now be criticised as not paying sufficient attention to the needs of the child, that we would give an equal welcome to a child of any ethnicity. We would have thought it racist to prefer to adopt a white child, and at the time it would have been seen as such by many people we knew. The adoptive parents needed, of course, to have a positive attitude to helping the child understand their culture of origin. The policy of "same-race" placement, by this time well aired in the United States, was only just beginning to be discussed in Britain and did not guide our thinking.

We had thought only as far as how we would help a child understand and belong to his or her own ethnic group. To be "colour blind" seemed to us to deny an obvious difference, not simply about skin colour but also about history and culture. We planned to acknowledge the difference and to think about what it meant. We probably underestimated how poorly situated we were to achieve this, living as we did in a largely white community, even in a city with a large minority ethnic population.

We had also discussed the question of religion. Tom and I are not religious, so we could not promise to bring up a child in accordance with a particular faith, but at the same time we respect the beliefs of others and would not have tried to prevent a child from developing their own.

Then there was the question of who would look after the child. It did not seem fair for both of us to continue working full-time, making a distressed toddler adapt not only to new parents but to accept child care arrangements as well. Tom had just started a new job as a social work lecturer, whereas I had been in my social work job for some time. That, and the greater social effort that a man at home with a child would have to make, meant it was easier for me to give up work.

Hearing, after some months, that we had been accepted as

adoptive parents, we began to look forward, with a mixture of trepidation and impatience, to the stage where we could start to think about a real child. The first child discussed with us was five, older than we had wanted. But it was not long before our social worker brought reports about two other children who needed a home. One was a dual heritage two-year-old boy, and the other was a black girl, Rita, then aged seventeen months. Jackie was not asking us to choose between them, merely wondering what we thought. We were interested in both children.

We might have spent the next few weeks wondering which of these children would join us. Instead, we sank into gloom, arguing over trifling matters. Suddenly, the last thing we wanted to do was take in some strange child who would invade our space and change our lives irrevocably. Yet, after as little as a week, the mood passed. On her next visit, Jackie was unperturbed to hear our tale – it was apparently a common reaction. Like many welcome changes, what was about to happen would bring some regrets.

> *This time, Jackie wanted to talk about Rita, who had spent the first few weeks of life at home with her single parent, Cynthia, and her brother, Danny, who was nearly two when she was born. Cynthia and Rita were then admitted to the mother and baby unit of a psychiatric hospital as Cynthia's mental health worsened and, shortly after that, Rita went to live with the Clarks. She had now lived with them for over a year and was progressing well for her age. Cynthia had experienced earlier episodes of severe mental illness and her chances of recovery were thought to be slim, so social workers decided to place Rita for adoption.*
>
> *Cynthia had not wanted Rita taken into care and was not prepared to agree to adoption. At the time, Danny, who shared the same father with Rita, was three-and-a-half and living in a children's home. As a*

result of her illness, Cynthia had neglected Danny seriously but this had only become evident after Rita was born. The local authority had assumed parental rights over both children.

Jackie explained that Cynthia had once appealed unsuccessfully in the juvenile court for the return of her children. She had the right to appeal again and could win. She could claim that her neglect of Danny was not wilful, but due to her illness at the time. Nothing seemed worse to us than for Rita to become part of our family and then to return to her mother. She would have to undergo all the insecurity of yet another change.

Tom and I also had to consider how we felt about the possibility of Rita inheriting Cynthia's illness. We had talked generally about mental illness and adoption. Now we were facing the reality.

Danny and Rita's putative father, Jackson Graham, apparently wanted custody of his children. As DNA testing had not then been introduced, he could not prove paternity. To the best of the social workers' knowledge, he had never looked after or maintained the children, so his claim was thought weak.

In line with our views, we felt positive about the fact that Rita was black. With the benefit of experience, I now think we were not in a position to think through or tackle the issues in any real depth. We simply planned to do our best.

As to Rita's other circumstances, we had to decide quickly how much we were prepared to take on and try to anticipate what could happen in the future. Jackie advised us to think carefully about Rita and offered to arrange a meeting, should we wish. She also explained that she was leaving her job and that our new social worker would be Sarah. We thanked her for the part she had played in helping us to become a family.

That night, we thought over what we had discussed with

Jackie. We had never expected adoption to be easy or straightforward and we decided we were prepared to take on a challenge. The next day I rang the adoption unit to say we should love to meet Rita.

2

Rita arrives

On a sunny May morning, a day to match my feeling of hope, I set out to bring Rita home. She was standing in the Clarks' sitting room as I arrived, a small figure next to a large plastic bag containing her clothes and toys. The day that meant so much to Tom and me held no particular significance for her. She greeted me with a bright smile as Sandie and I collected her things together.

'Goodbye, Sandie. I'll give you a ring in a couple of days to let you know how Rita is settling in,' I said. I knew that Sandie would think it intrusive to contact me, but she would want news of the little girl she had nurtured since babyhood.

Rita waved cheerfully as we drove away. When we got home, she ran into the house and stood first in the kitchen, her face bright with pleasure and recognition. She dashed from room to room, stopping briefly to tear open one or two waiting presents, and ate her lunch with enthusiasm.

After lunch, we scattered toys around and played happily, but later on, Rita's mood changed. She became ominously quiet. I tried to distract her, but she was less and less interested. Leaving the toys, she went up to the closed door of the sitting room and placed both her hands on the knob. She twisted it uselessly and soon her hands dropped helplessly to her sides.

'Car! Car!' she said, and then came a long cry of 'Mummy!'

I could see that tears were not far away. Tom's arrival home provided some diversion, but when we made no move to put Rita in the car, she gave way at last and cried persistently. Nothing we tried would persuade her to stop. She sat on my knee while Tom crept around the kitchen making helpful drinks. Then, as if exhausted, she quietened down and, with infantile resilience, stayed up brightly until eleven o'clock in the evening. We were definitely the worse for wear.

The next morning, after Tom had left for work, I took Rita out in the pushchair and she did not seem at all distressed. After lunch, she slept and it was well into the afternoon before she woke. A peaceful half hour ensued and then she must have thought again about going home. She climbed onto a chair and banged on the windowpane.

'Mummy, Mummy! Car! Car!' she cried, ignoring my attempts to distract her. Tears streaked her face as she repeated her plea. I lifted her down and tried to comfort her and again she cried for hours, refusing consolation.

That evening, Tom and I began to introduce a new routine. We thought that bedtime at eleven at night was too late for Rita and had decided to advance it gradually, so she would not notice the change. It was well after eleven o'clock before she fell asleep that night but, to our relief, our plan worked eventually. Accompanied by some protest, Rita was not only in bed by seven o'clock in the evening within three weeks, but would tolerate being left alone in her cot and was sleeping in her own room. Tom and I had our evenings back again and Rita had a suitable routine. Feeling a twinge of guilt for making more changes in Rita's life, I gave away some of her clothes to make way for things we had bought. This was part of claiming her as our child.

The next few weeks repeated the pattern of the first two

days. Rita did not lose her appetite, but she cried frequently. Standing on the armchair crying out 'Mummy' and 'Car' became almost a daily activity. We comforted her as best we could.

I rang Sandie several times, both to let her know how Rita was getting on and for advice. After all, Sandie knew her best in those early days. She explained little things about Rita's likes and dislikes that were new to us.

We were all convinced that Rita needed to continue seeing the Clarks so that she would know they had not abandoned her. They were to come to us for the first visit, to show that they knew where she was and approved. This was preferable to our taking her back to her old home and misleading her into thinking that she was returning to live there.

Sandie and her husband arrived one Saturday afternoon four weeks after Rita came to us. Rita answered the door with me. She was thrilled to see who was standing there. They came in and we all watched Rita to see how she would react.

'Mummy! Mummy!' Rita said softly, kneeling on the sofa by Sandie, her face beaming.

Sandie was visibly affected and looked at Rita as if she did not know whether to smile or cry. She saved the moment by diving into her bag and pulling out a little parcel. Rita glowed at seeing the long white nightdress inside. She put it on straightaway and danced around the room.

It was a relief to talk to the people who knew Rita well and obviously cared for her. We assured the Clarks that Rita had missed them, but was getting used to us, and told them – almost as if they were fond grandparents – of all the little things she had said and done.

At the gate, as we waved goodbye with Rita in my arms, I felt her body suddenly lurch towards Sandie and then settle back against me. She may have expected to go back with the Clarks and then realised that this was not going to happen. That small movement reminded me that Rita was not yet our child. But in one way, I felt reassured. Rita had learned to love and trust and her affections were not to be lightly regarded.

Everyone was wrong about the time it would take Rita to love us both as her parents. Despite being social workers, neither Tom nor I knew much about how children respond in such circumstances. We had been showered with advice by many professionals, friends and relatives who said that she was young enough to settle in quickly – within a few weeks – and we had seen no reason to dispute it. In fact, it took many months.

Rita offered no contradiction, at a superficial level, to the received wisdom because she co-operated so well with her day-to-day routine. Life with her lost its mint newness after the first visit from the Clarks. Gradually she cried less from the distress of leaving them, and more often from being tired or thwarted. She continued to sleep and eat well and was often curious and eager. We began to think she would accept us. We breathed more easily and felt a growing sense of confidence that we could cope with her from day to day. Much of the time Rita was delightful, with the ready smile and trusting manner of a happy infant. People melted at seeing her face wreathed in smiles.

Tom was euphoric to find Rita in his life. He took to fatherhood with ease and assurance. He showered her with affection, delighted in teaching her anything, and his pride in her was evident whenever we introduced her to anyone. He never corrected her in more than the gentlest of tones. Rita reciprocated. When Tom left for work in the morning, she turned to me and said, 'Daddy gone'. When he came home in the evening she gave him an enormous welcome, running to the door, clamouring to be picked up and shouting 'Daddy! Daddy!'

With Tom out at work all day, it was not long before I began to feel that chance contact with neighbours and visits from friends and relatives was not enough to sustain

Rita and me through the course of the day. She needed children of her own age to play with. One morning we set off to find a local playgroup, run by mothers for pre-school children in a large church basement. As we entered, we saw toddlers running everywhere while their mothers chatted in small groups. Rita sprinted away to explore the climbing frame, painting table and toys. A neighbour introduced me to one or two people and, feeling rather conspicuous because Rita was so obviously not my child in the ordinary sense, I embarked on explanations.

Rita and I began to attend the playgroup two mornings a week. I was pleased to see she was enjoying herself, but disconcerted that she rarely seemed to need me. Other mothers complained that their children clung to them, while Rita was always busy at the other side of the hall. At the end of the session, we sat in a circle to sing nursery rhymes, toddlers on their mother's knees. But Rita refused to sit with me. I knew it would take time for her to accept me, so I threw myself into working for the playgroup – making coffee, clearing up, opening up in the morning. I talked to as many of the mothers as I could meet. Our earliest friend was Carol. She had a little daughter of Rita's age called Katy. On discovering a mutual enthusiasm for swimming, we started to take the girls swimming every week. Rita loved the water and developed a passion for it that lasted throughout her childhood.

Although we lived in a largely white community, I did not have to look far to begin helping Rita to nurture her ethnic identity. Our immediate neighbours were a family of mixed African and African-Caribbean origin, with two children older than Rita. When Alice, the mother, saw Rita over the fence one day, I introduced her. Alice offered to plait Rita's hair. I oiled her skin every day and used coconut oil on her hair, but I brushed it lightly for fear of hurting her, and this had resulted in a mass of tangles.

Alice came in one morning, armed with a tin of grease, and set to work with Rita on her knee. Rita cried and struggled to get down. Alice murmured soothingly as her brush and comb teased their way through the tangles. It looked painful and it was not long before Rita began to howl. Both Alice and her daughter had assured me earlier that it never hurt them to do their hair, but they did not have such tangles. Alice managed half a head of plaits before we decided Rita had had enough.

Later that same day, I finished the plaits, painstakingly adopting Alice's approach and trying to be as gentle as possible. Rita cried throughout, but I persisted because I felt I owed her a proper hairstyle. When I showed her the results in a mirror, she was thrilled. A little hand crept up to her hair and she touched with surprise and pleasure the plaits that sprouted from her head. I took her next door to show Alice and we both made a lot of fuss of her.

Despite Alice's example, I did not plait Rita's hair again for a long time as it seemed to hurt too much and took so long. Isolated as I was from much daily contact with black people, I did not notice that Rita, with her untouched curls, looked an oddity in the eyes of black parents. It was not long before we met a black parent, Rita's mother, Cynthia, with some views very different from our own.

3

Exploring differences

Tom and I wanted to find out as much as we could about Cynthia so that we could help Rita to know her mother. Jackie told us a bit about Cynthia's story.

Cynthia's parents came to England from Jamaica when she was a baby, leaving her there in the care of a godmother. When Cynthia was about eleven, her parents sent for her, and so she came to England to live with parents whom she could not remember. Several younger brothers and sisters had been born in England and Cynthia was now one of twelve children. She did not achieve her potential at school in England and left without qualifications. We heard that her relationship with her parents was poor at the time: perhaps she was too homesick to fit into her new family. As an adolescent, Cynthia suffered bouts of depression.

In her early twenties, Cynthia met Jackson, who was of the same age. Like Cynthia, he had spent his early years in Jamaica, coming to England with his parents and family when he was about eight years old. When their son Danny was born, Cynthia was given a council flat. Jackson did not move in with her, but

and directed her attention again to the battered nursery collection. In all this time, Cynthia had said nothing to Rita and the rest of us had done little more than make encouraging comments about the presents. Tom said afterwards that he felt embarrassed that so many people were taking part in what for Cynthia must have been a very private occasion. Cynthia gave little indication of her feelings for Rita, and Rita for her part did not seem to recognise her mother after a gap of many months.

Cynthia's manner conveyed emptiness, almost as if no one were there. She did not seem cold, just absent. We felt our way, trying hard not to dominate. Cynthia asked no questions at all about Rita. Finally, Rita, bored with the toys, crawled onto Tom's knee.

Jennifer then turned to Cynthia. 'I know you have one or two questions to ask. Perhaps you would like to ask them now.'

Cynthia looked across to us. Breaking her long silence, she asked me abruptly, 'Do you believe in God?'

'No,' I replied.

The already enormous gulf between us widened further. No one had asked me this question for years, not since I was an adolescent struggling to work out my beliefs. Fortunately, Tom came to the rescue.

'We don't believe in God,' he said, 'and so we don't belong to any kind of church. Our beliefs are humanist and we intend to bring Rita up to be honest and kind and good to others.'

'But she should believe in God and go to church! She should read the Bible!' Cynthia was astounded. Rita was pushing trucks around our feet.

'She will learn about religion,' I said. 'There's religious education at school and we can talk to her about what religion means to people. But we can't teach her to believe in God when we have no faith ourselves.'

'Will you stop her going to church if she wants to go?'

We promised never to prevent Rita from going to church if she wished to go.

Cynthia changed tack. 'Are you going to have another child to stay with you?'

Tom replied that we had not really thought about it yet. We wanted Rita to be thoroughly settled first.

Cynthia persisted. 'What about a boy? Older than Rita.'

'We would probably want a younger child because it would be hard for Rita to accept an older child,' I replied, steering the conversation away from Danny as I knew the social workers had other plans for him. Clearly he was on Cynthia's mind.

Cynthia would not give up, nor would she come out into the open. 'There must be a boy a bit older than Rita, who needs a home,' she said. Then suddenly she changed the subject again. 'Is Rita obedient? She must obey you.'

'Well, yes, I suppose so. If you ask her to stop doing something, she usually listens,' I replied.

'I can see you are modern parents. A child must obey her parents and this will be easier if she is brought up as a Christian,' said Cynthia.

Cynthia had not told us directly that she would not consent to the adoption, but she had confided to Jennifer earlier that she was opposed to it. After meeting her, and despite her oblique references to wanting a home for Danny, we were certain that she would not willingly sign the adoption papers.

We made an agreement with Sarah and Jennifer that Cynthia could see Rita every three months, now that Rita was settled with us, and prior to her adoption. It was important to show the court that Cynthia had not been treated harshly by the local authority. Refusing her access could have been construed as harsh treatment. The local authority was planning to ask the court to dispense with Cynthia's consent to adoption on the grounds that she was withholding it unreasonably. Their case would rest on the fact that Cynthia was not able to care for Rita, that Rita was settled and thriving in her new home, and that it was in her interests to stay there. They argued that it would be difficult to assert that Cynthia was withholding her consent unreasonably if she had not been able to see Rita at all. It did not seem to us that this would necessarily be the case, but we had no reason to argue the point as we had already agreed that Rita would benefit from seeing Cynthia.

Three months after the first visit, I took Rita to see Cynthia again. Once more there were sweets and presents, this time clockwork toys with sharp metal edges, which Rita could not possibly have operated herself. Again, Cynthia must have been thinking of Danny when she bought them.

On this occasion, Cynthia had the same stillness and her manner lacked ordinary warmth, but her mood seemed better. She tried persistently to convert me to her religious views and almost ignored Rita. She quoted parables and the Bible and found it impossible to accept that I had a different approach.

'Would you seek revenge on someone who wronged you?' she asked.

'No, but I might seek justice through the law,' I replied.

'You should always revenge yourself on someone who has done you wrong,' Cynthia said fiercely.

For the first time in many years, I found myself explaining my values and beliefs, without endeavouring to hide from Cynthia that they were different from her own. Only after this lengthy conversation did Cynthia take much notice of Rita. She sat her on her lap, and produced a copy of a magazine for black people.

'These are black people, Rita, and you are black, not white. You will grow up to be like them. See, here is a black man. He is handsome and successful and here is a beautiful black woman.'

I watched Rita looking attentively at the pictures. Despite her being too ill to care for her children, Cynthia had something valuable to teach Rita about her culture and heritage. I was not to know then that Cynthia's wish for her children to be together would soon be fulfilled.

4

Finding Danny

The Clarks came to see Rita for a second time after she had lived with us for six months. Rita knew them instantly. Her memory, which was excellent, was helped by the album of photos they had given her when she left them and which she loved to look through. But this time, her response was different. Now, instead of rushing to Sandie, she hung back. She sat like a stone, too young to ask questions, yet too old to have forgotten her past. The Clarks were sympathetic and treated her gently. As soon as they left, Rita reverted to her normally bright mood.

About this time, an event occurred which changed our lives. We attended a reception for foster parents, including those like us who were fostering with a view to adoption. It was hosted by the local mayor and addressed by the head of the local authority adoption and fostering service, who spoke about "children who wait". Everyone present was circulated with a list of these children who had waited a long time for a permanent family. Such children were "hard to place": many of them were older or disabled. Several were black. The speaker pleaded with us, as existing foster parents, to consider these children, as few babies and toddlers of any ethnic origin were available for fostering and adoption. We had thought Rita would like a younger brother or sister. Now it seemed as if this would be difficult to achieve.

Back at home, we started looking at the list of "children who wait". Nearly forty children were featured, all in the care of the local authority. Each name was followed by a paragraph of description. With no thought in mind apart from curiosity, I read aloud to Tom, starting from the beginning. Soon I had read out the details of so many children, that I stopped looking at the names. I found myself reading about a small boy, much younger than most of the children on the list.

'He is a good looking and lovable little boy, tall and sturdy for his age. He has very large brown eyes and short black hair and a mid-brown complexion. He has a happy personality, though he has a clear will of his own. He loves his bike and the climbing frame and is very agile. He is always on the go. He seems to be an intelligent child and he really enjoys life to the full. He has been in a children's home for eighteen months. His mother was mentally ill and while she had the care of him, he developed severe rickets and was greatly under-stimulated. He has caught up in his development thanks to the care he has received, but his house-parents want him to have the chance of a real family life. He needs a permanent family as soon as possible and foster parents would be able to adopt him in due course.'

I glanced idly at the name. 'Danny! Why, he must be Rita's brother. Look!' My voice rose with excitement as I passed the list to Tom.

'Let's see if we can meet him,' Tom said. 'He sounds like such a lively, active boy – so different from everything we have heard before about him.'

The social workers had told us of a plan to foster Danny with a family where he would be the only child so he could have unrivalled attention. They thought he needed to be alone with new parents after all the deprivation he had endured.

The more we thought about it, the better it seemed for Danny and Rita to live together. They would not feel alone in facing their circumstances as they grew old enough to understand why they had been taken from Cynthia. Each child would be company for the other and Danny would feel more at home with us than with other parents, because he would be living with his sister as well.

We thought back to what Sarah had told us about Danny when describing Rita's family background. This is her story, as we remember it.

> It wasn't until Cynthia was admitted to hospital to give birth to Rita that it was discovered that Danny was in a very neglected condition. For this reason, parental rights were taken away from Cynthia and she was no longer permitted to have the care of her children. Cynthia had kept Danny indoors all the time, on a diet of cereal with no milk or other dairy foods or any meat, fruit or vegetables. As a result, he developed severe rickets.
>
> On coming into care when Rita was born and he was nearly two years old, Danny could not walk unaided and his ankle and wrist joints were very swollen. He was a year behind in general development. It seemed that Cynthia had rarely dressed him. She had left him in his cot or sat him on her lap and cuddled him. She was not in any way deliberately cruel, but she had no idea of how to talk to or play with him or interest him in the world around. Danny's condition was so serious that after only two days in a children's home, he was admitted to hospital where he stayed for a month receiving treatment for rickets and for the first time experiencing a varied diet. Until then, no health visitor, social worker or GP had seen Danny since he was five months old.

'It's astounding that Danny escaped notice so completely and for such a long time,' Tom said.

'What about his own family?' I asked.

Sarah explained further. 'As far as we know, Jackson saw Danny as a baby, but has never met Rita. His parents live locally and his mother asked to foster Danny and Rita, when they came into care.'

I was puzzled. 'Well, that seems rather a good idea. Why didn't you agree?'

'Because Cynthia disliked Jackson by that stage and we thought that placing the children with his parents could have led to conflict.'

'But all families have conflicts, and maybe Cynthia would have preferred that to seeing her children adopted out of her sight,' said Tom.

'Well, there was another reason. We also felt that Jackson's mother was too strict to have the children.'

Tom and I did not comment further as this decision had been made some time ago. We both felt uneasy, however, about the social worker's judgement that had prevented Danny and Rita from living with their family.

The story went on.

After his month in hospital, Danny was discharged home to live with Cynthia and Rita. Within a few weeks, Cynthia became ill again and she and Rita were admitted to the psychiatric hospital. Danny went to a residential children's nursery. He spent a few months there and was then transferred to a children's home. He can run around and talk, but has still not fully recovered from the effects of rickets. His development is still below average for his age. The plan is to place him for adoption with a family where he will be the only child, because he needs a lot of attention. If Danny and Rita were to live together, Rita would quickly outstrip Danny in her general progress and undermine his confidence.

Seated in our kitchen all these months later, we reasoned that Danny must have made a lot of progress in the last year to merit such a favourable description in the list of children waiting for a new family. We had no reason to suspect that the description fell misleadingly short of the truth – the author, who was in charge of the children's home where he lived, wrote from a desire to do her best for him. Danny had made tremendous strides, but he had not overcome the disadvantages of his early years.

Fired by our decision to meet Danny, I rang Sarah the next day. She liked the idea, but sounded a note of warning. Apparently the head of the children's home and her husband were thinking of fostering him.

'But we want to meet Danny anyway,' I argued. 'We've talked it over and we think that Rita should have a chance to know him and he needs to know her.'

Sarah promised to talk to Danny's social worker. Three months passed before we heard any more. In the meantime, there was plenty to occupy us at home. Rita's first birthday party with us, when she was two, saw Tom playing the piano for a roomful of parents and children as we sang nursery rhymes. At one point, Rita decided to play the piano with him. Realising the tune was not right, she took one of Tom's fingers and tried to play the piano with it. She was puzzled that she could not produce a tune. Everyone laughed and Rita laughed with them, delighted with her audience.

My friend Carol and I had taken on the task of organising the playgroup Christmas party. Exhausted but still on our feet by the appointed day, we were relieved that it went well. The entire assembly sang nursery rhymes, conducted by one of the mothers. Cakes and jellies were thrown around with great energy and the appearance of Father Christmas caused the usual mixture of excitement and fear. Rita cried and clung while I was busy serving food. When we returned to the kitchen to fill more plates, I sat her on a table with a chocolate biscuit, and sped on with my task. Whether having such a scant portion of my attention made her look at me with new eyes, I shall never know, but she suddenly said to me 'I love you.' It was her first loving or affectionate remark to me and I treasured the moment.

A shower of presents greeted Rita at Christmas. Everyone we knew had taken her to heart. Tom's parents, who lived nearby, were delighted by Rita and slipped easily into the role of adoring grandparents, praising and enjoying her every action. My parents, who lived further away and had less opportunity to see Rita, welcomed her too.

Shortly after Christmas, Rita came out of nappies. It seemed to happen quickly and she was pleased with herself. The fact that we had missed her first eighteen months gave me the curious feeling that her life was telescoped. It was a feeling that returned each time she took some major step forward, as if her childhood were happening too quickly.

By this stage in her life, Rita was a lively and talkative child. Changing families had not apparently marred her ability to learn at all. She took words up with zest and repeated them hundreds of times before she relegated them to everyday use. She loved words for their sound as well as their meaning, and would repeat a new word with force and a broad grin. Then, at just two, she began to string words together to make sentences. We told ourselves that if Rita could give so much energy to learning after living with us for only six months, then she had a chance of being a reasonably secure and happy child.

We took Rita to the Clarks for her first visit since leaving their home eight months previously. She was quiet at first and looked uncertainly at the family circle gathered for the occasion. Then she broke into movement and ran around, climbing into her old pram and teasing the cat.

At the end of the visit, she came away with us happily, calling in with Sandie to see the neighbours on the way.

Half the street seemed to collect around her as people exclaimed about how she had grown and pressed pocket money into her hand.

After she had lived with us for about nine months, Rita began to show more affection for me. Disappointment when I appeared instead of Tom was replaced by pleasure at seeing me. She chose to play with me sometimes when we were out visiting instead of rushing off to whoever else was around. Rita began to seem like our child in the fullest possible sense; she was proudly and lovingly possessive of her parents. No child born to us could have been loved and wanted more.

We continued to see the Clarks every six months or so until about the time Rita started nursery school at three. She appeared to suffer no after effects from the visits and despite awkward patches, would always start to chatter again, like a clockwork toy suddenly wound up, after the visit was over. We stopped when it seemed no longer necessary. Rita was well past babyhood and she was by then settled into her daily life with us. But before then, a big change was to occur in Rita's life: the arrival of Danny.

5

Enter Danny

Once again, Tom and I found ourselves facing a door, which would open to reveal a child we hoped would join our family. This time, Rita was with us, and if the visit went well, we were hoping to offer Danny, now aged four, not only parents, but a sister as well. It was a winter afternoon about eight months after Rita's arrival. We stood waiting, wondering what Danny, who had lived here for nearly two years, would be like.

Since deciding to meet Danny, we had talked to Sarah and met Marion, who ran the children's home and who had cared for Danny more than anyone else since he had left Cynthia. Marion had written the description that had ignited our interest in him. We had formed the impression that Marion was devoted to Danny, although Sarah had assured us that she and her husband had finally decided not to foster him, because they were to take on another boy from the children's home who had been there much longer than Danny. We had also read an affectionate and lively description by Marion of Danny's daily life in the children's home and a doctor's report. Danny had recovered well from early deprivation, but his speech was indistinct because rickets had caused his front teeth to fall out at the age of three, just at the time when he was learning to talk.

When Marion, a fair-haired, solidly built young woman, came to the door, she said little as she asked us to come in. She led the way into a sitting room where several children, except for Danny who was asleep upstairs, were half-heartedly watching ice-skating on television. We introduced ourselves while Marion disappeared. It was some time before she returned, carrying Danny. She sat down and cradled him closely in her arms while we peered across, trying to see him and yet somehow prevented from doing so.

'Hello, Danny,' Tom said brightly as he introduced us. 'This is your sister Rita. We are sure you want to see her so we have brought her along this afternoon.'

Danny said nothing. He did not resemble Rita at all, in manner or appearance. My mind flashed back to our first meeting with Rita and her lively presence in the Clarks' sitting room. Danny was big for his age, an attractive looking boy, with large eyes and the longest eyelashes I have ever seen. He was sleepy and for the first hour he scarcely noticed Rita. His gaze wandered slowly around the room, while he clung to Marion.

Eventually, Danny gravitated towards Tom, whose easy manner appeals to children. We stayed for a rather uncomfortable tea. Marion struggled hard to make small talk, but our presence was inhibiting for the other children. I sat next to Danny, mesmerised by his appetite. He devoured a stream of sandwiches and cakes with a concentration that left no time for conversation.

After tea, as if fuelled, Danny livened up. He smiled and jumped around, a toothless grin almost splitting his face in half as he played with Rita's teddy bear.

'What colour is that teddy bear's suit?' Tom asked him at one point. Danny examined the red suit carefully.

'White,' he answered. Other questions, put gently, revealed that Danny could not identify any colours correctly and had little vocabulary. But I felt I had made some contact with him.

On the way home, we exchanged impressions. Danny was an appealing boy, but Rita had taught us that absorbing a child into the family is a slow process requiring endless patience and love. We thought Danny was too attached to Marion to welcome a new mother, but he would perhaps want a father and a sister. He had undoubtedly made progress with Marion, but he seemed inexperienced for his age. On the other hand, he was able to lead a normal life and would be unlikely to deprive Rita of too much of our time and attention, as would be the case with a seriously disabled child. We came to the decision that we wanted to offer Danny a home and told ourselves with a superficial wisdom that it would take him a year or two to settle in. As Marion and her husband were not going to foster Danny, Sarah agreed when we contacted her that his best chance was to grow up with Rita.

Danny had not been fooled by a visit from his sister. He sensed that change was in the air. We heard later that after we left, he turned to Marion and said: 'Am I going to live with them?'

'Would you like that, Danny?'

'No!'

Together with Marion and the social workers, we planned Danny's introduction to our home. He would move in with us in three months' time and we would prepare him by seeing him regularly and building up to Danny visiting our home. Finally, he would spend a weekend with us before moving in. The mechanics of Danny's move were well organised, while his emotional ties, the seeds of later troubles, were less thoroughly considered. Nobody, not the social workers, nor Marion, nor even Tom and I, really listened to what Danny was saying. He was, after all, only four years old and his views about his future could not be the deciding factor.

Shortly after the decision was made about Danny, Rita

and I met Cynthia, with Jennifer. I told Cynthia the news, remembering her earlier indirect questions about Danny. I stressed the fact that her children would be together. I did not expect her to approve, and she said little now, but she nodded her head.

Cynthia was not taking any medication at this point, but she seemed lethargic. She was looking increasingly thin and had given up her job as a messenger. Marion reported that she found Cynthia's behaviour odd when taking Danny to see her. Cynthia had apparently wanted Danny to sit on her lap for the entire visit and had asked him repeatedly if he loved her. Danny had squirmed and tried to wriggle away.

Danny's introduction to us was held up for some weeks by illness in the children's home and we were asked not to visit him. Rita had joined us only five weeks after we first heard about her, yet seven months elapsed between our first seeing Danny's name on the "children who wait" list and his moving in. When our visits resumed, it was clear that he did remember us, but with foreboding. He told Marion that he did not want a new mummy and daddy. We thought we understood his unwillingness to move, but we did not suspect the strength of his feelings.

Marion came with Danny on his first visit to us. He brought his teddy bear, which he was to leave as a sign that he would be coming back, and so that he would have a well-known toy of his own when he visited again. We showed Rita's bedroom to Danny.

'Now, where would you like to put your teddy bear, Danny?' Marion said. Danny's room was not yet ready for him.

'There!' he replied, sitting his worn brown bear on Rita's chair.

'No!' shouted Rita, throwing it on the floor. A struggle ensued and the teddy bear was left rather uncertainly in the room, while we distracted Rita's attention. Tom and I hoped Rita would be more welcoming as time passed.

For his next visit, we collected Danny and brought him back alone. He accompanied us with a wooden obedience, but in the presence of Rita's infectious high spirits, he gradually came to life. The only other sign of distress he showed was that he wet himself rather than go to the bathroom in time.

In the afternoon, an incident occurred which left us in no doubt about how Rita felt. One of her favourite occupations at the time was to play the piano with Tom. Hearing the piano, she ran in from the garden to find Danny in her place. Tears flowed as she fought for her usual seat.

'No room for Danny! No room for Danny!' she shouted as she pushed him away from Tom despite her pint size, and installed herself firmly on the piano stool. Danny was dumbfounded and had no thought of fighting back.

Rita took up this little slogan and used it liberally over the period of Danny's introduction and for the first few weeks after he moved in with us. 'No room for Danny!' she would chant if he wanted the last piece of cake or as she snatched one of her toys from him. Accepting a strange four-year-old boy into her life must have been harder than accepting a baby would have been. A baby would not have been older and bigger or taken her toys. On the other hand, Danny offered companionship and required less physical care from us than a baby. In more merciful moments, she loved playing with him.

About this time, Sarah was asked to see a Mrs Graham, who had applied to the local authority to become a foster parent. Sarah discovered that Mrs Graham was Danny and Rita's paternal grandmother. This was the same grandmother that Danny's social worker had been reluctant to place him with on account of her being "too strict". Whereas Mrs Graham had not been allowed to foster Danny and Rita two years previously, she was now being accepted by Sarah as a possible foster parent for other children. It was not simply that Sarah took a different view from the social worker who had dealt with Mrs Graham's application to foster Danny and Rita. Around us, things were changing. In the two years between 1979 and 1981, social workers were developing a stronger commitment to finding black families for black children in need, and a better understanding of what black families have to offer. We followed the debate about the needs of black children closely and we agreed with the policy of "same-race" placements, if a matched family could be found after a reasonable amount of searching, because it is easier for children to belong to a family with similar characteristics to their birth family. This change in policy fuelled our own commitment to helping the children develop relationships with their birth families.

The time came for Danny to stay overnight with us. He had asked for a bedroom of his own like Rita, and was pleased that he could have it. His overnight stay was uneventful. We talked to him about his move to us and tried to make it sound real, safe and fun. He said little and Rita, at two-and-a-half, could not really be prepared for future events. The stage was set, as far as possible, for Danny's entrance.

6

Distress

Rita raced into the hall on hearing a knock at the front door.

'It's Danny!' she cried as we welcomed the new arrival.

Danny arrived with Marion and a substantial array of luggage and presents. He was moving in and now he spread everything around him in the sitting room: a new two-wheeler bike, an enormous trolley of bricks, a large truck with passengers and a money box shaped like a policeman, all from Marion. There were the remains of an enormous cake she had made, shaped like our house, with tile-red icing on the roof and the number on the door. She had also opened a bank account for Danny.

Then there were the presents from other people: games, boats, cars and a football. Danny also had books several years too old for him, which were past presents from Cynthia, inscribed with her love in the now familiar black capitals.

'We had a big party for Danny with lots of children from nearby,' said Marion, as she handed round photographs of the event.

'And I've got a bike. It was a surprise.' Danny rode it proudly around the room.

'We blindfolded Danny and led him to the bike,' Marion added. Danny was in an energetic and excitable mood. He was enjoying the moment and was apparently forgetful of its significance. He gave no hint of the distress, tears and misery that were to follow, and it was not until much later that he confided in us how he had dealt with having to leave Marion – by pretending that he was coming to us for only one night.

Danny let Marion go without protest. Playing once again with his presents after she left, he accidentally caused Rita to cry. I picked Rita up to comfort her and Danny collapsed into even louder crying. It took Tom and me half an hour to calm him down.

'I want my Marion, I...I want my Marion!' Danny wailed. Similar scenes occurred many times over the next days, weeks and months. Danny longed for Marion and was obviously puzzled by his move to us.

Two days after Danny arrived, I rang Marion to let her have news of him and to give him an opportunity to talk to her. We had decided he should go on having contact with her without a long break, so that he would be reassured that she had not disappeared and know that she still loved him. Danny talked on the phone to Marion, naming the children he had left behind and listening to her voice.

'Why?... Why?... Why?...' he kept saying, unable to finish his question. He seemed to be asking why he had to leave Marion, a question he soon learned to ask in full and to repeat frequently.

Marion came to lunch at the end of Danny's first week with us. Before her arrival, Danny dissected the photo album which she had given him and spread the pictures of the children at his children's home on the chairs and floor of our sitting room as if to say 'These photos represent my real life'.

He was thrilled to see Marion. Perhaps he thought or hoped that she had come to take him home. I was careful to give him time alone with her while I distracted Rita.

Marion brought with her the story of Danny's life so far. She had written it in clear print in a book with hard covers and in a style a small child could easily understand. She had even visited Cynthia to check some facts about Danny's early years. Danny was entranced as she read it to him.

The story contained a description of Jackson and Cynthia, pictures of Jamaica, a careful account of why Danny had to leave Cynthia, and details of his life in the children's home. Both Danny and Rita were intrigued by the fact that the book was about Danny and pored over the photos and drawings. After Danny learned to read, it was one of the few books that he would read to himself.

The visit went well until Marion got up to leave. As Danny watched her put on her coat, he started to cry and then to sob desperately, until he was totally out of control. This was the moment he realised that there was no going back to Marion. Danny's behaviour inevitably prevented Marion from leaving, as it was intended to do. She fluttered anxiously around him, becoming upset herself. Then Rita's face crumpled into tears.

'Marion, I am sorry, but it's best that you go,' I said. 'If Danny thinks he can keep you here by crying, then we aren't going to be able to calm him down.'

Marion nodded wordlessly. She was crying openly now and tears streaked her face as she ran from the house. The full force of what we had done hit me too. I felt as if we had torn Danny away from the person he had regarded as his mother; the one person he had found to trust in all the unhappiness and disarray of the first four years of his life. It seemed impossible that we could ever enable him to become a loving and trusting member of our family. At that moment it would have been so easy to call out to Marion and return her child to her; after all, Danny had just demonstrated, with tremendous force, that he was her child.

But Marion was gone and my immediate task was to

calm Danny. Sitting him on my knee only made him wilder and he struggled free. For more than half an hour he screamed hysterically, while I tried uselessly to comfort him as his rage and despair ran its course. Rita stood by aghast. Her performances were no match for this. In the end, we took Danny up to bed, where he sank into an exhausted sleep.

Danny made it clear in many ways that he wanted to go back to Marion. At first, every time anything went wrong, he reacted in the same way. His mouth drooped and pouted, his face crumpled and he started to cry.

'I don't like you! I don't like you! I want my Marion!'

'I'm going...I'm going to get a mocabike' he said one day. 'And I'll ride away on it.'

'Where will you go?' asked Tom unsuspectingly.

'To Marion. I'll ride away to Marion.'

A month after her first visit to Danny, Marion came back, at our invitation. Danny had been asking for her steadily and we decided it would be better if he could see her, so that he would know she had not forgotten him. She brought four children from the children's home, but at first she and Danny only had eyes for each other. Sensing this, the other children became very demanding of her attention and did not allow Danny and Marion to behave as if no one else was there. The atmosphere of the visit was noisy and playful and Danny let Marion go without a scene.

That summer, Danny and Rita played together well on holiday, but we noticed how Danny allowed Rita to boss him around. He rarely spoke unless he wanted something or in answer to a direct question. One afternoon, I was swinging him around.

'Do you think about Marion, Danny?' He had not mentioned her recently.

'Yes.'

'Do you want to go and see her?'

'Yes.'

'What will you do there?'

'Have lunch and then I will play.'

'And then what?'

'Go home.'

We took this conversation to mean that Danny was beginning to accept that he lived with us. Encouraged, we arranged for Marion to visit Danny again. By now, he had been with us for three months. On her arrival, Danny clung to her wordlessly. They sat on the sofa together, Danny's dark head buried in her long, fair hair. Difficult as it was to see him clinging so desperately to Marion, while he was so reluctant to be with us, I realised Danny needed the comfort she gave him, a comfort which he would not accept easily from us. Only at tea time, and then to have a bath, did he climb down from her lap. As she left, he was splashing around in the bath and there was no scene. I was grateful for the peaceful ending to the visit.

After this visit, Tom and I decided that it would be better if Danny did not see Marion for a while. He seemed to be missing her too badly to be able to cope with his day-to-day life with us and it was not helping him to have the wound reopened. We were quite sure that he loved Marion as deeply as any son could love a mother, although we were aware that his distress at leaving her could stem from the earlier trauma of being taken from Cynthia. But he needed a chance to adjust to his life with us. We thought he could start again with Marion on a fresh footing at a later stage.

And so Marion did not see Danny for three months. Then, when he seemed a little more settled, we asked her to make a brief visit again. Danny was very pleased to see her and quite able to let her go. A few days later, we were sitting at the kitchen table at lunchtime. Rita had gone into the sitting room to play; Danny remained with us.

'Why do I need a mummy and daddy?' he asked.

'To look after you and love you. And you have a sister to play with as well,' answered Tom. We always emphasised Rita's presence when pointing out to Danny the advantages of family life as we hoped she was a powerful argument in our favour. This time, Danny had the confidence to answer back.

'I don't need a mummy and daddy. I could live at the children's home and I could be with Marion.'

'But, Danny, children don't stay in the children's home very long,' I argued. 'Marion has to find families for them, where they can be happy, with new parents to love them. All the children you were with have gone to families now.'

Danny looked unconvinced.

'We want you to stay with us, Danny, because we love you and this is your family now,' Tom said, giving Danny a hug as he spoke. 'You can still see Marion. And why don't you write to her? Tell me what to say and I'll write it down for you.' He fetched pen and paper, but Danny had lost interest. Writing a letter did not give him what he wanted.

'I had a nice lunch and a nice walk and a nice play,' he dictated in a bored voice.

Another time, I overheard Danny talking to Rita in the bath, as I passed the bathroom door.

'I'll cut Mummy up with a knife,' I heard him say. 'And put her down the plughole.'

I crept away, not knowing whether to laugh or cry. Danny's fantasy was to get rid of us and return to Marion. It may have compensated for an everyday life he did not accept.

It was difficult to decide how much time Danny needed to spend with Marion, but after discussing it at length, we decided he was ready to see more of her and we invited her to telephone or visit when she could. Danny might be over the painful stage of separation, but he kept asking about Marion and she still meant a great deal to him. It was important for him to see her. To refuse him any contact with her would have deprived him of the closest relationship he had ever had with anyone. We would also have prepared the ground for him to resent us even more and perhaps to prevent him from ever forming the close bond with us that he needed. That Marion was willing to encourage Danny to accept his new life was a considerable help to us.

We worked on the assumption that if Danny had developed a strong bond with Marion, he could in time achieve the same with us. If he still said that he wanted to go back to her, then this showed that he was capable of deep feelings. As time went on, we learned that Danny saw things rather differently. His view was that he had been forced to leave Marion and was expected to transfer his affections to virtual strangers. He was compliant for the most part, but he held on to the idea that he wanted to return to Marion and so he negotiated a position on the very edge of our family.

7

Danny at home

It took Danny a long time to adjust to living with us and in some ways he always maintained a certain distance. At teatime on the day he moved in with us, he ate desperately, shovelling in food as if he remembered his near starvation as a baby. The next morning, he resisted my efforts to dress him. He came downstairs and planted himself in front of me, looking up to catch my attention. I glanced down to discover that he had put all his clothes on back to front. Tom burst out laughing, but Danny did not quite see the joke. This was a serious attempt to make things difficult for us. Trying at that moment to do several things at once, I was inclined to agree that he had succeeded.

It was not long before we discovered other signs of distress. Danny was severely constipated; he soiled his pants daily; he was restless and could not concentrate on anything. He accepted a bedtime story because Rita always had one, but his fingers ruffled the pages anxiously as Tom or I was reading and he did not seem able to listen.

At first, Rita hated to see Danny getting attention, despite our making an extra fuss of her too. Noisy crying was her answer and she was not above thumping Danny when she felt like it. Danny never seemed to be angry with her, so they were evenly matched, with Rita making up in force of spirit what she lacked in size. Then Rita started wetting the bed. Apart from the occasional accident, she had by this time been perfectly dry for over a year. In the mornings, if her sheets were wet, she would lie in bed for as long as possible. If they were dry she would say brightly 'Look, Mummy, I haven't wet the bed!' and expect a reward. We had started to reward Danny for clean pants after school and Rita was not going to miss out. I threatened to move her back from her bed into her cot, from which she had graduated recently. This worked for a little while, but then she returned to regular bedwetting.

At the core of our concern over Danny in those first months was a feeling of dread that he would never accept us as his parents. We wondered if he had suffered lasting damage from the experience of his first two years and whether he would recover from the trauma of being taken first from Cynthia and then from Marion. He was an unhappy, distressed and insecure child who needed to be given time, affection and patience, but it was hard going, because he did not respond to warmth in the normal way.

Yet Danny had many endearing qualities. He was often tractable and easy going. He was usually ready to smile and always pleased to meet people. He never had to be persuaded to eat. He was helpful and often almost anxious to please. He was keen to tackle any physical challenge. At the beginning we had some reason to feel that he would adjust well.

Danny liked chasing or playing "mummies and daddies". He would take the part of the baby, leaving Rita, if friends were absent, to be a parent. He would lie helplessly on the floor, while she mothered him energetically by covering him in clothes and blankets. Only when persuaded would Danny play with Lego or draw, only when sitting with us would he ever look at a book. He could not tolerate his own company. Left to himself, he would stand on his head, chase breathlessly round the house or hang off a doorknob. He would not let Rita look at a book or draw or play on her own, and always interrupted her.

For weeks after Danny moved in, the merest setback caused him to cry for hours. On one occasion, I sent him up to his room because he was crying uncontrollably over some minor incident with Rita. Tom and I had agreed on this new approach to lengthy crying sessions. A few minutes isolation were sufficient to calm Danny down, while trying to comfort him only made matters worse. Danny stomped upstairs and banged his bedroom door shut again and again. There was a glass panel in the door and I was afraid he would break it and cut himself. I also knew that he had only recently watched us putting it in. I flew upstairs. Danny's face was awash with tears as he continued to slam the door. Without thinking, I smacked him and then, feeling guilty for losing my temper, left him to calm myself down. Danny had been with us such a short time and it could be years before he felt really settled with us. I went back again to make it up to him and quietly he let me take him downstairs.

Danny was over-eating. As it made him miserable if we tried to cut down on his food, we decided, for the moment at least, to let him eat his fill. We thought, rightly as it turned out, that his appetite would become more normal as he began to feel better in himself. So Danny was able to assuage his sorrow at losing Marion by continuing to eat enormous amounts of food. What he loved best at tea time after school, if he had friends to play, were large home-made wholemeal pancakes covered with melted cheese, with a generous layer of baked beans on top. One was enough for other children – Danny always had three.

Danny made mistakes in talking, and we thought he would learn by example. But it was hard to ignore when Rita, quick to copy him, also began to say "we was" or "the thing what you gave me". We noticed that he would also use a word similar in meaning or sound to the one he meant, for example, he always said 'beans' for 'peas,' his word for swan was 'pond' and needles were 'nails'. These oddities were different from the infantile speech he had retained and showed a difficulty in making the right distinctions between sounds or objects. Tests showed that there was nothing wrong with his hearing. Poor concentration, stemming from emotional confusion, was the more likely cause. He avoided using new words and his indistinct speech made him hard to understand. He did not listen and constantly had to ask us to repeat something. It seemed that speech was a last resort and he tried to make it as simple as possible. So, instead of saying 'Look at that bird sitting on the roof over there,' he would say 'Look at that, there.' He was better approached through activity or a hug than conversation.

Despite his appetite, Danny found that mealtimes posed a challenge. It was months before he could say simple words like jam or marmalade and he would point instead. At first we hardly noticed because we were too preoccupied with helping him feel at home, but at breakfast one day, I tried to encourage Danny to use the words for what he wanted.

'Ask for what you want, Danny,' I said, seeing him point at the jam just out of his reach and look at me, hoping that I would interpret his unspoken wish.

'That,' said Danny, still pointing at the jam.

'Ask for it properly, say what it is,' I persisted.

Danny stared at me mutely, knife poised, unwilling to risk a mistake. I gave in rather than push him as he seemed so fragile. He had to learn at his own pace. What had worked with Rita was totally wrong for him. Rita continued to absorb new words like a sponge, repeating them with a verbal flourish and dancing eyes.

Tom decided to persist with the word 'windmill,' which became a symbol for him of Danny's capacity to learn and his own skill in helping him. He talked about windmills, took Danny for walks to look at one nearby, and encouraged him to draw them. Danny learned to say the word when shown a picture of a windmill and started to draw them of his own accord. Later he even made a cardboard model of one.

Danny was also clumsy. He crashed into the furniture and flung Rita accidentally to the floor on many occasions. The use of small objects like Lego or pens and crayons was a struggle for him. At four-and-a-half, he was drawing like a child of two – possibly another legacy of early deprivation. He lacked experience with a lot of the materials young children commonly use in play. There had not been enough staff in the children's home to teach him about painting and plasticine, and Marion had been unwilling to let him go to the local playgroup. She had seen him as too frail, which was true when he first came to her, but he became stronger under her care.

I bought an array of art supplies, jigsaw puzzles and games based on shaping and sorting. I arranged everything in boxes and on shelves so Danny could help himself when he wanted to. Rita enjoyed helping me sort it all out and after school I enticed Danny to experiment. He always needed encouragement, but within months he was beginning to add details like facial features to his drawings and to use more than the colour brown.

On the warm summer days in Danny's first months with us, I let the children shower themselves in the garden with a hose. I made large cushions for Danny to bounce on indoors and took him to the park with Rita after school – he loved the children's playground there. I invited other children to tea, as I did for Rita. At the weekends we would take the children out as much as possible.

Danny continued soiling. At first I thought he was anxious about asking for the toilet away from home, but then he began to soil regularly at home as well. He was constipated and this caused him severe discomfort. One morning he was in pain and I rang the doctor who advised syrup of figs. It was Sunday and there were few shops open and none which sold syrup of figs. Tom invited our neighbour, Alice, to come in and she made hot sennapod tea. Danny drank it and the pain disappeared.

Soon after that incident, Danny saw a paediatrician for a routine examination, part of the follow-up after his hospital admission at the age of two. The paediatrician diagnosed chronic constipation, of which the soiling was a symptom. He thought the most likely cause was anxiety over leaving the children's home and coming to live with us and that it would probably take Danny a long time to recover. He prescribed a strong daily dose of laxative initially and later an enema, which was administered in the hospital. It caused Danny to scream but was very effective and the regular doses of the laxative helped. Danny had eczema, which slowly abated and then disappeared, but his skin seemed very sensitive. He hated being cold and in his first winter with us would cry excessively if we went for a walk in the cold weather.

Danny liked meeting people and our friends were gratified by his approach to them. He would go up and ask for a "cuggle" from anyone he met. He smiled confidingly, held hands or launched himself energetically on receptive adults. People did not realise he was indiscriminately affectionate and simply saw him as a charming little boy. They thought we were taking on a challenge, but they were encouraging and optimistic. Other mothers invited him to tea. Carol remarked on how much her daughter Katy liked Danny and we noticed how kind he was to younger children.

Danny made a friend called Zach, a solemn little boy of the same age, who lived in the next street from us with his black mother, Amber, his white step-father and his step-sister and a dog who always seemed to be tied up somewhere and protested by barking until released. Amber noticed me taking Danny to school and asked me to take Zach as well. It was no trouble to take one extra child. It was not long before Danny wanted Zach to stay to tea and then not long before he stayed to tea on most days. He was a polite boy, whose solemnity gave way, when he was amused, to a huge smile and a great shout of laughter.

The autumn half-term meant a change in routine and Danny, who loved going to school, sulked his way through the week. He kicked aimlessly through fallen leaves in the park and dragged behind us on walks. He did the same at Christmas.

I was tired, and yet sleeping badly. At about five every morning, having fought against wakefulness for about two hours, I would fall asleep again. At six, as regularly as the dawn chorus, Danny would awake and sing or chant repetitively outside our bedroom door. I pleaded with him to play quietly when he woke up, but he could not bear to be alone and even a disgruntled mother was better than the silence of the house. We were beginning to realise we had taken on far more than we had expected and had to acknowledge that Danny was not happy with us and that we were struggling with him.

And Rita? She had changed since Danny's arrival. She cried more and no longer welcomed people effusively, but was more inclined to be shy. At home she alternated between bright and dark moods. Her ready grasp of language and quick response perhaps obscured her reaction to the changed family structure. We felt that she had gained a lot from Danny's company, but his arrival had forced her to stand back and learn to share. Now when Tom and I gave each other a hug, there were two children joining in.

Danny loved his first birthday party with us, when he reached the age of five. Zach and several other boys came. Danny joined in the games, ate enormous quantities of food and, although he was a little uncertain about how to behave when other children won prizes, he thanked me beautifully afterwards for giving the party for him.

With the experience of Rita taking time to accept me, I could let Danny's coolness towards us wash over me more easily. Rita, on the other hand, had idolised Tom from the start and his first experience of rejection came with Danny. One Sunday evening, when I was in the kitchen at home, Tom took the children upstairs to put them to bed. Suddenly I heard him roaring at Danny, whose wails followed. I raced upstairs to find Rita looking scared and Danny howling.

'He just doesn't talk! I asked him a simple question, three times, and he completely ignored me!' Unused to anger, Tom seemed more upset than Danny.

I offered to look after Katy once a week while Carol was working. At nearly three, she was a good-natured and lively little girl with a rich imagination and a great capacity for getting along well with other children. She was funny and entertaining and we all enjoyed her company. Katy and Rita stood in the bay window of our sitting room one day, singing the alphabet clearly and perfectly. Danny had tried to learn it too and now he echoed them 'A... B...C...' He tailed off, adding a few letters at random. Living with Rita, two years younger and in some ways so much more advanced, was not easy for him. Neither Danny nor Rita ever commented on this and Danny seemed able to learn from Rita without loss of self-esteem. We missed Carol and Katy when they moved away not long afterwards.

Rita developed into a mimic at three. Since Danny's arrival, she had tried to get attention by raising her voice or radiating charm or crying. Now she began to copy Danny, shaping her mouth to suggest her teeth were missing and delivering words so inaudibly that it was necessary to bend down to hear her. At first it was amusing and then it began to seem as if we had two children with speech problems instead of only one. But as always, Rita was ahead of us and she moved on to mimic a friend. However, for the most part, Rita was a loving, rewarding and amusing child. People took to her. We were impressed by her creative use of language. At three, she said to me one day 'Mummy, my mouth is dizzy from so much talking!' One day, on a walk, we came across some beehives, and Rita, recognising them from pictures, said straightaway 'Look – there's a honey hutch!'

Danny and Rita were by now beginning to get along well. Brief arguments would flare up now and then, but Rita's early jealousy was fading and there was, after all, some room for Danny in her life. She learned to write his name as she learned to write her own and the nursery teacher commented that Rita thought a great deal of her big brother. They shared toys and baths with enjoyment and good humour, but they still competed over us. I would walk to school with a child's hand in each of mine, Danny stumbling slowly through sentences and Rita's voice rising higher and higher as she tried to drown his.

When I was alone with him, Danny seemed a most companionable child. He liked to potter around the kitchen and showed a touching desire to please. He loved to dry the dishes, a task he performed with enthusiasm and some mishaps. No one struggled with the rubbish bin or hauled the shopping trolley with more effort than he did. He looked injured if I forgot to ask him to put out the milk bottles. His physical superiority to Rita was of vital importance to him. One day for some reason I threatened, not very seriously, that he might have to go without tea and immediately he cried out 'That's not fair! Rita will get bigger'n me and I will be small!'

After a year with us, Danny began to be affectionate in a way that was less demanding. I was sitting on a low wall in the garden at home, talking to a friend, one summer afternoon, when Danny came to sit next to me and put his arm round me. Surprised and touched by this spontaneous show of affection, so different from his normal style of launching his body heavily on me and clinging on to my neck to the point of strangulation, I put my arm round him.

Danny still said he wanted to go back to Marion and that it was wrong to have to live with a mummy and daddy, but he was beginning to belong to us. All the cuddles, all the night-time kisses he had submitted to, all the times I had held his reluctant hand on the way home from school, had sown their seed. Perhaps even our irritation helped him to feel wanted. Tom and I began to feel more optimistic. Danny still woke us up at an early hour in the morning; he never spontaneously picked up a book or a pen; he still hung off doorknobs and crashed around the house. At five-and-a-half, he found life possible without the alphabet, he had no concept of time and could not use words like tomorrow or yesterday. But he was changing. He was even occasionally heard to say 'no' to more food. He was a little taller, slimmer and clearer eyed. We relaxed and everyone close to us noticed the change in Danny.

Danny was good at jigsaw puzzles and they were the surest way to get him to concentrate. And, one day, he surprised me when we were playing a game which required a good visual memory. He excelled and beat me easily. He left us in no doubt of his success. 'I'm a clever boy! I'm a clever boy!' he shouted, thumping his chest. It was delightful to see him so pleased and confident. But before he reached this stage, he had to get to grips with a new and demanding world – the world of school.

8

Off to school

Tom and I felt Danny needed as much time at home with us as possible before engaging with the outside world. However, it soon became clear that he wanted to be out of the house and did not consider us as necessary for more than providing food, clothing and shelter. In his first week, he asked to go to school so often that in the end we agreed.

Within a week of his arrival, therefore, Danny started attending the nursery class of a nearby primary school. It was June and the school wanted him to go into the reception class in September, the beginning of the term in which he would be five. I argued that he needed more time in the nursery and it was decided that he should stay there until Christmas.

Danny went eagerly to the nursery on his first day. Refusing to let me through the gates, he dashed into the playground without a backward look. Rita and I waved in vain as he vanished through the door. I watched the other mothers taking their children in to help them settle. To Danny's disgust, I collected him before the morning session ended, by agreement with the teacher, as part of his introduction. He wanted to have a school dinner and not suffer the humiliation of being led away to dinner at home with his baby sister. He dragged his feet and would not meet my eye or say hello.

'Hello, Danny, how are you? Have you had a good time at school – what have you been up to?'

'Not telling you,' Danny growled, looking away.

He trailed behind us and I waited for him at every corner, calling to him to catch us up. When I made him walk by our side, he cried for the remainder of the journey. The next day, a similar story unfolded. After yet another performance of this kind on the way home a week later, Danny collapsed into the house in a heap and lay howling on the floor. He fought me as I tried to pick him up, so I left him alone. He lay crying and sobbing on the floor for two hours and only as his cries subsided would he let me touch him. He was as limp as a sleeping baby by then and let me comfort him.

The nursery teacher told us that Danny's vocabulary was limited, his verbal reasoning good, his drawings immature and his concentration fleeting. He was sometimes sulky and unco-operative at school; he was soiling frequently; he had difficulty using the small toys and shapes that help children to make the fine movements that are a preparation for reading and writing. He would only use brown paint. He demanded a lot of affection and clung to adults inappropriately for his age. Fortunately, she added that she had every confidence that Danny would make good progress.

At the beginning of the spring term, Danny moved to the first year infant class and could look down on the nursery as fit only for babies like Rita. He skipped to school on the first day, a little ahead of me.

'I'm going to have just one lunch, not two lunches. You don't want a boy to have dirty pants, do you?'

Rita started to attend the nursery class just after Danny moved to the infants. As a leaving present for the playgroup, we bought a black doll to add to their collection of white dolls. It was always difficult buying black dolls.

The best one we could find, after a long search, was only a half-hearted grey colour, with straight hair.

Rita was thrilled to have her own life outside home. Almost from the first day, she would rush into the nursery every morning and then turn to me and say, 'I want you to go home now'. She had learned from Danny to show independence. But once the novelty had worn off, she liked me to stay for a few minutes to watch her playing. She told me in great detail about her activities in the nursery, which I found most refreshing after Danny's usual 'not telling you'.

I met one of the other mothers, Marcia, whose son went to the same nursery. Marcia offered to plait Rita's hair, so one afternoon we went to her house. Marcia and her husband had emigrated to Britain from Jamaica, and all her children had been born here. She seemed unsettled and talked about going home. She was worried about the Britain her children were growing up in and wondered if they would be discriminated against when they were older. She listened with interest to the story of how Rita came to live with us and was surprised that she had not remained with relatives.

Marcia spent a careful hour making many tiny, neat plaits. As she had with Alice, who had by now moved away with her family, Rita screamed her way through the session and I sat on the edge of my chair, torn between wanting to spare her distress and wanting her to be like other little black girls. Marcia assured me that doing their hair did not hurt her two daughters and that once it was properly untangled, it would be easier to comb through. Rita was thrilled with her plaits. For a week, they looked neat. Then back we went to Marcia's house to eat home-roasted peanuts and plait Rita's hair again. The screams were less piercing this time.

I began to plait Rita's hair every week myself, and went on doing it, with some short breaks, every Sunday night for years. It always took a couple of hours, with protests not uncommon. The challenge was to not make Rita cry. Week by week the little plaits grew longer and the tears fewer. Rita was always happy when the moment came to look in the mirror at her finished head of hair.

Meanwhile, Danny began to do well in the infants. He was lucky to be in a small class and his teacher was patient and encouraging. We made it clear that we were pleased with him. I had earlier explained to the teacher that we did not expect Danny to make progress at school while he was still absorbing the changes in his life. She agreed. She also cleaned him up when necessary and I was grateful to her for this help.

Then Danny discovered the school club, run by the teaching staff after school for the children of working parents. He was keen to stay on after school, like Zach. Tom and I felt it made too long a day for Danny in his first year, given that he had so little experience of family life. But Danny did not want to be at home. Every afternoon when I collected him from school he would say, 'Can I stay to club?' I continued to refuse and made sure he had plenty of friends to play with at home.

The parents organised a summer disco at school when Danny was five. Rita was too young to go, but Danny loved the flashing lights and loud music. We scarcely saw him the whole evening except when he came to us for hot dogs and crisps. He positioned himself as close to the speakers as possible and danced for hours.

'My old nursery teacher came all across the room to dance with me!' he told us afterwards, his face beaming.

Danny was worried about going back to school for his second year. He had thought school was entirely for fun, but now he realised that something more was being expected of him, something that he did not like and that he referred to as 'hard work'. He called himself 'stupid' because he found the work harder than most of the children in his class. He quickly dissolved into tears if we tried helping him with schoolwork at home.

'I don't want to do sums or writing. I don't want to read,' he complained one day, just after the beginning of the autumn term, as he climbed the stairs with Tom on his way to bed.

'You can spend money more easily if you learn to count, and read stories to yourself if you learn to read, and you can write your own letters to Marion.'

Danny pouted. 'No. I don't want to go to school.'

'All your friends are there and you like playing with them.'

'I can't play. I only know chasing.'

It was rare for Danny to express his lack of confidence so directly. His teacher (who had moved up with the class) asked to see me one day. Danny was not keeping up with the rest of the children. He did not like school work and would finish it in a great rush, then sit and play with something else. While standing by her desk to read, he would fiddle constantly with her papers. He would disturb other children, rather than attend to his work. He had been placed with a younger group for number work, because, at almost six, he could hardly count and was not ready to start sums. His memory was poor and he was clumsy.

Danny's teacher recommended more educational games at home, although this had to be approached with care because Danny resented our trying to teach him anything, and was already feeling under pressure. The games at home had to be seen as fun rather than connected with school. We also talked about increasing Danny's time at the after school club. We had decided at the beginning of term to let him stay one afternoon a week for football practice and now it seemed a good idea to let him stay another afternoon for quiet games in the classroom.

I was sobered by this session with Danny's teacher. Talking about it later, Tom and I decided Danny needed psychological testing to identify specific problems in his learning. But when I asked the head teacher to refer him to the School Psychological Service, I was told not to be over-anxious and that other children were in far greater need of help. The truth was that the service could not cope with the demands being placed on it.

Danny began the second half of the autumn term of his second year at school badly. He soiled every day, but rather than admit what had happened, he would stuff his soiled pants into his pockets. Then suddenly he stopped soiling altogether. Whether it was the result of the laxative the paediatrician had prescribed or whether he cared about the complaints his classmates and friends were beginning to make about him, was impossible to tell. And one afternoon, for the first time, he came up to me with a smile and a greeting after school. He changed his attitude to reading and learning at home and allowed us to teach him in the evenings sometimes. One boost to his self-esteem came from the fact that he was big and strong for his age – other boys would refer to this with respect.

Danny sometimes wondered if he would grow up to be white like Tom, but otherwise had never, by the age of five, talked about his colour. At seven, however, he complained occasionally that he was called "chocolate" and "blackie" at school. A game of "chase the chocolate" had been briefly popular amongst the boys in his class. The school dealt promptly with racist name-calling and the teachers explained to the children why it was wrong. We encouraged Danny also to point out that it was wrong and to enlist his teacher's help, but not to retaliate with insults himself.

After he had lived with us for eighteen months, Danny's continued allegiance to Marion led to a crisis of confidence for me, during a half-term week. I felt unable to finish more than the simplest household task. I acknowledged my strong wish for Danny to return to live with Marion. Eighteen months of struggle seemed enough. Although by then we were starting to plan for legal adoption of both children, in this mood, I found it hard to imagine. I told myself I did not want a reluctant child in our home. He was still Marion's child. Despite my efforts not to,

I caught myself snapping irritably at Danny. Two thoughts preoccupied me: Danny's slowness was frustrating, and I found it hard to live with his rejection of us.

I needed to do something, so I rang Marion. Because we had been away for the summer and she had not taken up an earlier invitation to visit, we had not seen her for six months. On the phone, Marion talked much more freely about Danny. She told me why she and her husband had decided not to foster him. They had thought he needed a full-time mother, rather than one who ran a children's home as well. Then there was the opportunity to grow up with Rita – a great point in favour of Danny's coming to live with us. I asked Marion to come and see Danny as I felt he needed her explicit permission to be adopted by us. She offered to come the next day.

In the rough and tumble of the children chasing around the house after her arrival, I managed to talk to Marion. We both agreed that no one, least of all Danny and Marion herself, had realised how close their relationship had been. Marion added that she did not regret giving Danny up, but I remembered the time that she had visited us and left the house in tears.

Danny was joyous at seeing Marion again and spoke in an unusually coherent manner after she left. On his return from work that evening, Tom was astonished at how fluently Danny talked to him. Danny was eagerly looking forward to a night at Marion's house, a plan of his own concoction, for which he had secured everyone's agreement. He spent two weekends, some months apart, with Marion, returning from both in fine spirits. The first was a short overnight stay. He told his teacher and friends about it. His teacher was now someone he could talk to about Marion, and this must have helped his world to become more coherent. He planned the second weekend as soon as he came home from the first. Staying with Marion seemed to give him the strength to adapt to a new life.

My period of crisis over Danny ended. Sarah, our social

worker, was phlegmatic and said it was common for parents to feel like this at some point before an adoption, but she was wise enough not to dismiss my feelings as mere butterflies. I was able to believe that Danny was making progress, to hope he would learn to love us and to continue trying to accept him as he was. I doubted if Danny had noticed any difference. I was ready, and so was Tom, to go ahead and adopt both children. But first, we were to see Cynthia in a much more disturbing light.

9

Cynthia's fury

Shortly after Danny joined us, I took Rita to meet Cynthia again. Danny was at school. He and Marion had seen Cynthia recently and he was to have three months to get to know us before seeing her again. He never mentioned her of his own accord. He seemed too busy coping with the loss of Marion and adjusting to his new world.

On arrival at the residential nursery, Rita gave herself up to the delights of having an entire playroom to herself. Jennifer and Cynthia were late. When Cynthia swept in, attired from head to foot in flowing black, with a scarf around her head, she scooped Rita up without a word and carried her to the other end of the room. She sat down with Rita on her knee, ignoring my greeting.

'You see, Rita, that is not your mother. Look at your skin. It is black, like mine. You belong to me, to us, not to that evil white woman. She will teach you bad ways, cut your hair and treat you badly. Look, Rita! You have scratches on your leg. You are marked. What has she been doing to you?'

Rita stared. I was alarmed by Cynthia's words and the new, angry note in her voice. Jennifer whispered her apologies for being late. She had gone early to Cynthia's flat to talk to her and Cynthia had become agitated, raging against the people who had caused her to lose her children. Jennifer had been frightened and wished she were sitting nearer the door so she could make a swift escape. Trying to calm Cynthia only seemed to make her worse. Finally she had induced Cynthia to get in the car and they had driven down to meet us.

Falling silent, but making no attempt to play with Rita, Cynthia eventually came over and stood near me. She refused to sit and stood looking down at me.

'Danny has moved in with us now,' I said in an attempt to diffuse the tension in the room and remembering Cynthia's earlier wish that the children should be together.

'Oh, of course, you will bring him up to be like you as well. You will force him to think like you.'

I could not think of a useful reply and Cynthia turned away from me to the window. She began to mutter to herself and to pace up and down. Rita was playing by herself all this time. As I had to go and collect Danny from school, I stood up and Cynthia handed me a bag of presents for the children.

'Thank you. That's very kind,' I said.

'You dare to thank me!' snapped Cynthia. 'How dare you! I am their mother, not you. Therefore, I have the right to give them anything, with no thanks. I am no stranger who must be thanked for a gift!'

I turned away and with relief set off with Rita to collect Danny from school. I spared a thought for Jennifer taking Cynthia back to her flat, and hoped that Cynthia would remain calm.

At home that evening, Tom and I examined the bag of toys. There were eight large packets of toffees and a green plastic truck on which Cynthia had inscribed with indelible ink 'TO MY DARLING DAUGHTER RITA WITH ALL MY LOVE FROM YOUR LOVING MOTHER CYNTHIA' and a few other little plastic toys. The truck did not last very long. The inscription seemed to catch my eye all the time and I was glad when it fell to pieces.

There was no sign that Rita had been adversely affected by this meeting, although Tom was concerned to hear of our experience. Once or twice in the weeks that followed, Rita draped a scarf around her head and, looking up with a mischievous smile, said, 'I'm Cynthia'.

Autumn had scarcely begun when it was time for another visit to Cynthia. Both Danny and Rita were to see her this time. I had not forgotten her mood in the summer, and told myself not to make a fuss, but underneath I was frightened. Tom wanted to come with me in case Cynthia was still angry, but it would have meant his taking an afternoon off work. I assured him we would be perfectly all right.

It was a warm September afternoon and Danny enjoyed the walk to the residential nursery, while Rita perched on my back in her carrier. We were shown into a playroom where Rita settled on a rocking horse. Jennifer and Cynthia arrived a few moments later. This time Cynthia was dressed conventionally in a raincoat and skirt. Tea arrived and she refused it. She barely talked to the children and seemed to have broken her habit of bringing them sweets and presents. Danny made a noise with a drum.

'Be quiet, Danny!' Cynthia snapped.

I started to drink my tea. Cynthia came and sat near me. Jennifer was at the other end of the room, as were the children. Cynthia opened a Bible she had brought and read out the parable of the vineyard and the three sons in a loud voice. My feeling of dread meant I scarcely heard the words. Cynthia read quickly and as she finished, she raised her voice to a shout.

'And now perhaps you will understand that my children are mine and not for you to take away and bring up by your standards!'

She was shouting loudly now and as she finished, she leapt up and across the room at speed. Almost before I could move, she had pushed Jennifer backwards onto a low table and locked her hands around her throat.

'Cynthia, no!' I screamed as I jumped up. I seemed to move like a snail after her, my voice weak and my legs heavy. I pulled her off Jennifer, whose frightened face stared up at me. Cynthia swung round and clamped her hands around my throat, only to be pulled back by Jennifer, who had staggered to her feet.

I had time now for the briefest glance at the children. Danny stood rooted and silent; Rita had collapsed into loud crying. Cynthia grabbed Jennifer again, hands around her throat a second time, and again I forced her free. Cynthia's arms flailed towards me and knocked my glasses off. I caught them and put them on.

Cynthia's hands clamped around my throat again, her fingers pressing against the back of my neck. I whirled my arms, forcing her to let me go, while Jennifer pulled at her from behind. I screamed for help. We could have overpowered and held Cynthia down in that moment, but somehow we did not and now there was a space between us all and Cynthia had stopped attacking us. We were all panting silently.

I stood, shielding the children, Jennifer near me. Cynthia snatched a child's recorder from the table and brandishing it like a weapon, harangued us. That she was speaking, I hoped, meant that she had finished attacking us.

'Unless my children are returned to my doorstep tonight, I will kill two social workers!'

We said nothing. I could not move to comfort the children until help arrived, because Cynthia might suddenly attack Jennifer.

The door burst open to reveal the matron and her deputy. They both suddenly looked small and frail. The deputy whisked the children away. Cynthia was calmer now and was led from the room. Only then did I feel free to attend to the children. I found them in a side room, Danny shaking and Rita still crying.

In a few moments, the deputy matron had bundled us out of the building and into her car. I had time for only a wordless look at Jennifer. Cynthia stood scowling by Jennifer's car, one elbow leaning on the roof, as if she were expecting a lift home. The police were standing near the door, no doubt called by the matron when she heard my shouts.

In the car on the way home, I tried to console the children. The deputy matron had taken a briskly reassuring attitude. She described other occasions when parents had been violent and the police called. I was grateful for her efforts, even if she did unwittingly give the impression that violent parents were a common feature of life at the nursery.

Back at home, Danny and Rita were calmer. It was hard to look at them and put into words what they had seen. I was ashamed of the fact that they had witnessed such violence when I was their protector. I tried talking, but my words seemed dull and lifeless and they did not understand me.

'Why were you fighting, Mummy?' Rita kept saying, as if I had started it.

'They should let me live with Cynthia. She would be kind to me,' Danny said. He had understood that she would never have attacked him. She had been fighting for him.

That evening, Jennifer rang.

'Thanks for coming to my rescue,' she said. 'I was convinced that my last moment had come this afternoon!'

We both made light of the incident, but it had not been funny. It scarcely needed voicing that our visits to Cynthia had come to an end.

'I'm afraid I've got a confession to make,' Jennifer said. 'A few months ago, I accidentally used your surname to Cynthia. I hoped my mistake went unnoticed, but several weeks later, Cynthia repeated the name, in conversation.'

The intention was that Cynthia should not know our

surname, or our address, so that she could not trace us to our house. Now we would be easy to find as she already knew the name of the area we lived in and no one else with our surname was listed in the telephone directory which covered it. It might not occur to her to try, but I felt uneasy at the idea.

The thought of seeing Cynthia again was certainly enough to make me quail. For two days after the incident, my body was tense with readiness to rebuff unexpected attack. A few weeks later, I was coming home from the playgroup with Rita, when she pointed suddenly and called out 'Look! Cynthia!' I forced myself to look across the road. A black woman was walking towards us. Older and of a different build, she resembled Cynthia only in colour. In the months that followed, I had several nightmares in which Cynthia would rush into the house, brandishing scissors or a knife and make for the bed where I was lying helpless. Or in the dream, she would try to take one of the children and I would struggle to prevent her.

Some days later, we learned that the police had taken Cynthia to the local psychiatric hospital. She had been left sitting unattended in a room on her own and, not surprisingly, had simply got up and walked out, returning to her flat. Later, she was invited to the social workers' offices where it was explained to her that she would not be permitted to see the children again as her behaviour had been harmful to them. She was told her only recourse against this decision was through the courts, but chose not to pursue this.

Rita was only a couple of months short of her third birthday at the time and she might easily have forgotten the incident quickly. Instead, she surprised us by remembering it for a long time afterwards and, although we never talked about it in front of the children unless they mentioned it, she was adamant in her refusal to see Cynthia again. Danny made no such fuss, and appeared to forget what had happened after a few months, but neither did he ever ask to see Cynthia. She had become too shadowy a figure in his life.

Several months later, we had a string of mysterious phone calls. At first, they came daily. The phone would ring, always in the afternoon, and I would answer. There would be a short silence and the caller would hang up. It was such an odd way for anyone to behave that we could not help imagining Cynthia sitting at home, brooding over the children and ringing our number in the hope that one of them would answer. The calls served to keep alive my memory of the last time I had seen Cynthia, but never became quite worrying enough for us to change our number. After about three months, they stopped altogether.

Tom would occasionally see Cynthia in the street when he was driving home from work as she lived only a few miles away from us. Dressed from head to foot in either black or white, she would walk along as if in a dream while people hurried past her.

We did not try to banish Cynthia from Danny's and Rita's minds. We had a photograph that she had given us and we would talk about her from time to time. Both children accepted the fact that she was ill and that they could not live with her. We had gone as far as we could with Cynthia at present. Now we had to turn our attention to a new factor – Jackson and his family.

10

Opening up

Cynthia had one or two short spells in hospital, where she responded well. Once home, she would stop taking her medication and her strange behaviour would return. At one point, she wrote to the social workers saying she had married her doctor and that he was the father of Danny and Rita. The doctor telephoned Jennifer because Cynthia was haunting his surgery, painting slogans on the wall outside. Jennifer felt that there was nothing she could do, as Cynthia did not consider herself to be ill. Jennifer told us that Cynthia was to be seen tramping the streets near her home, picking up rubbish from the streets. We felt sorry to hear this, because she was Danny and Rita's mother, and someone of significance for us.

Cynthia was inevitably not looking after herself properly. She fell into arrears with her rent. When a housing official visited, she raged at him senselessly, frightening him away. She refused to sign for receipt of benefits and a social security officer went to see her, only to receive abuse in turn. Unless she signed the forms, she could not continue to receive benefits and so her payments were stopped. She had no way of supporting herself, so she started visiting Mrs Graham, Jackson's mother, and eating with the Graham family. She was thin and starving. With a tight budget, Mrs Graham could not afford to feed Cynthia all the time. She asked Jennifer to help and eventually, Cynthia's benefit was restored. Not long afterwards, she at last began to accept medication.

Then, four years after Danny and Rita had been taken from Cynthia and just as we were preparing our court case to adopt them, Jackson turned up in the social workers' office. He was no longer in touch with Cynthia, except that he sometimes saw her by chance when visiting his parents, the Grahams. He had married, bought a house and set himself up in the business of house renovation. With a wife, a home and a reasonable income, he had decided to ask for his children as well.

Jennifer told him that as he had not been married to the children's mother and had not supported the children regularly, his rights were weak. She also said that she thought it would be wrong to move Danny and Rita at this stage, when Rita was settled with us and Danny in great need of security. As she talked to Jackson, Jennifer decided that he was more concerned that the children should think well of him, and to show that he could offer them a home than to have custody. She sensed the urging of Mrs Graham behind his sudden appearance.

We agreed that the children should have limited contact with Jackson, as he was their birth father. They would never then need to spin fantasies about him. Increasingly conscious of how limited was our ability to introduce Danny and Rita to black culture, we reasoned that Jackson and his family would be able to hand on the family history to the children and help them to develop and take pride in their ethnic identity.

Jennifer arranged for us to take the children to see Jackson one afternoon at the residential nursery. Danny and Rita wore their smartest clothes, their skin glowed and Rita's hair was newly plaited. Jackson was punctual. He came confidently into the room, a tall, heavily built, well-dressed and handsome young man, smiling and with hand outstretched. He had brought a large black teddy bear for Rita and a battery controlled car, with flashing lights, for Danny. The children greeted him politely as they did any stranger. He was one of many people we had introduced them to and the word "father" which we used for him appeared to mean little to them at the time. Jackson made little fuss of them at first. He had come to tell us about himself and he talked at length. This is his story.

> *I started by just seeing Cynthia now and then. It wasn't a regular thing. We didn't plan on having Danny and we were still really not much older than children ourselves when he was born – in our early twenties. When I found out Cynthia was pregnant, I thought I would marry her. But then after the baby was born, she was in such a rage all the time, she wouldn't agree to it. She wouldn't even see me, the father of her child! It wasn't long before they gave her a council flat where she could live with Danny. She still didn't want to see me. I used to give her some money – she made me feel that was all she wanted from me.*

Like Danny, Jackson spoke slowly. He laughed easily with a deprecating shrug. He said he had tried countless times to see Cynthia when Danny was first born, but had always been refused entry to their flat.

> *At first, I didn't even know Cynthia's address. Once I found out where she was, I would go round there and knock at the door and call through the letterbox. She would scream at me sometimes, but other times she let me in. I gave her lots of money for the baby. She used to leave him alone in the flat while she went out in the evenings.*

Later on, the relationship obviously improved, because

Jackson was positive that he was Rita's father as well. Cynthia's attitude had changed.

'She wanted to be with me all the time, like glue to paper,' he said. 'But I didn't see any future in it myself. She was too fierce, just too fierce for me.'

Jackson told many anecdotes of Cynthia's wrath towards him, even while she wanted him to stay with her. Most of the time he sounded tolerant. But on one question, he was adamant.

'Cynthia must never have the children back again. She didn't look after Danny properly. She doesn't mean any harm, but she can't manage it.'

'I want Danny and Rita to live with me now, but my wife wants us to have our own children and I don't think she wants Danny and Rita to turn up from my past. She is afraid of Cynthia, even though she's never met her – Cynthia and my wife are like cat and fish. But I want to see Danny and Rita sometimes.'

'Well, we thought you would want that,' Tom said. 'We think that it would be a good idea for them to know you and to know you want to see them now and then.'

'Of course, it wouldn't be every week – I'm very busy,' Jackson said quickly. In fact, we did not envisage his seeing Danny and Rita more than once or twice a year, at least until they were older.

We were struck by the similarity between Danny and his father. Not only did they look alike, but their manner was similar. Jackson had charm. We wondered how much Danny would resemble him in character, despite their different circumstances.

Two weeks later, we returned to the nursery to meet Mr and Mrs Graham. In the four years since Danny and Rita had left Cynthia, Mrs Graham had often asked the social workers for news of them. We had agreed to her request to see her grandchildren, because it seemed wrong to deny Danny and Rita their grandmother. Jackson, however, had asked to see the children without his mother present, so a separate arrangement had been made. Mrs Graham was heavily built, with a serious manner. Mr Graham, although not slim, was smaller. Like Jackson, he had an easy laugh, but he said little. It was clear from the beginning that Mrs Graham was the more powerful character. They both appeared really pleased to meet Danny and Rita and gave them a hug.

'Oh, look, you've done the child's hair nicely,' said Mrs Graham immediately. By that time I had advanced to cornrows and Rita's head that day was a neat radial system of plaits. Mrs Graham returned several times to the topic, explaining in detail how she did her own hair by plaiting it at night and brushing it out every day.

It did not take long for the conversation to turn to Cynthia. Mrs Graham confirmed that Cynthia had been very angry after Danny's birth and had refused to see anyone. She also said that Cynthia used to leave baby Danny alone in the flat when she went out.

'How are you getting along with Cynthia now?' I asked. Even though Cynthia was not a relative and was no longer seeing Jackson, she was visiting Mrs Graham several times a week.

'Well, she isn't looking after herself at all,' said Mrs Graham, heaving a sigh. 'She runs into the house when she comes round and straight for the kitchen to put the kettle on. Then I offer her some food because she's so thin. There isn't anything to her at all and she eats like a starving person. She doesn't cook in her flat because her gas is cut off – she doesn't pay bills. She couldn't buy any food because they stopped her Security, but it's back on again now. I really beat up my gum telling her to go to the Security, so in the end I took her there myself. She's looking after herself a little bit better now that it's back on again. But she doesn't wear warm clothes and her bare arms are frozen. She's wearing those long black and white clothes that she likes and they're so thin, it's no good at all. She shivers all through the winter.'

'Cynthia's forgotten about Danny and Rita. She never talks about them. It's a pity the court has to ask her about them. She shouldn't be allowed to see them or have anything to do with them again.'

Mrs Graham was firm on this point and Mr Graham nodded his agreement. We could not believe Cynthia had forgotten Danny and Rita, but perhaps she had given up hope of having them back, or knew that it would be too difficult for her to manage them.

Mr and Mrs Graham explained to us that they were originally from rural Jamaica and that, when they were young, they had worked on the land farming sugar cane. They came to England in about 1960, returning home for visits as often as they could afford to. They still had relatives and strong ties in Jamaica. They were worried that they might not be able to go again, as Mr Graham had been made redundant from his job with the Post Office. Now in his late fifties, he had not been able to find another job.

'I am glad Danny and Rita are with you,' said Mrs Graham. 'You asked for them and you could only do that out of love.' Tom and I exchanged looks. We felt uneasy – this statement seemed too well prepared.

'Now, we should like to see the children from time to time,' said Mrs Graham. Tom and I had already anticipated such a request and had privately agreed to it. As a sign of trust, we gave Mr and Mrs Graham our address and phone number. We were certain that they would not let Cynthia see it, but since Jennifer's confession, had some reason to believe that Cynthia already had that information.

'It was kind of you to see us and allow us to see the children. We never expected to see them at all,' said Mrs Graham. She and Mr Graham had expected to lose all contact with Danny and Rita through adoption. They gave Danny and Rita a generous present of money for toys as we parted and said goodbye to them with affection.

We debated afterwards whether the social workers had

made a mistake in not placing Danny and Rita with their grandparents. They would have been with their own family and ethnic group. These were powerful advantages and we did not feel we could reasonably dismiss them, even though the decision about adoption had been made a long time before Danny and Rita came to us and we had not been involved in it. We were simply living with its consequences. These thoughts influenced our decision to let the children see Jackson and their grandparents on a regular basis.

We were made very aware of the importance of religion to Mr and Mrs Graham when we met them again. They explained that they belonged to the Church of God and lived strictly by its beliefs, one of which was that the souls of people who were not saved would be damned and they would forever burn in hell. It was therefore of vital importance to save the souls of Danny and Rita. They also believed that every word of the Bible was literally true. Mrs Graham's faith tended to dictate the pattern of conversation. She would suddenly, and with no warning, switch from ordinary conversation to preaching, almost as if she were standing in a pulpit. We found it difficult to steer the conversation back into normal channels.

Mrs Graham explained that she wanted to take the children to church with her on Sundays. We agreed in principle, thinking this would be a good opportunity for Danny and Rita to meet more of their relatives, but said we wanted to wait until after the adoption hearing. We felt we had to get this hurdle out of the way before embarking on a new phase with Mr and Mrs Graham or Jackson.

The differences between us and Mr and Mrs Graham in our attitudes to bringing up children were demonstrated particularly clearly one day.

'The Bible says you must chastise the child,' Mrs Graham said, with the certainty of the believer.

'We would not say chastise,' said Tom, always a gentle and kindly father. 'If they are naughty, we reprimand them.'

'You must beat the child,' insisted Mrs Graham. 'Some people say you should raise the skin but we do not agree with that. What I mean is that if a child does something you have told him not to do, or if you ask him to do something several times and he will not, you must beat him.'

'I do smack them sometimes, if they make me cross,' I said, 'but some parents never smack their children because they think it is a form of assault.'

'Then they do not love their children, for if you never beat them, then they don't know how to obey you.'

Mrs Graham used the word "beat" as white people would have said "smack". She believed in teaching what she knew to be right, but she was not cruel.

One hot summer holiday, far from the influence of Mrs Graham, I cut Rita's hair. Rita was pleased with her short curls. Back home we went back to plaits as soon as Rita's hair was long enough. But as usual, she was one step ahead of me. She came downstairs one day with a very noticeable bald patch on the front of her head and a similar one at the back.

'It's Daddy's fault. He left the scissors in the bathroom.'

I cut Rita's hair again so that the bald patches were less conspicuous, which made it too short to plait. I had not calculated on the strength of Mrs Graham's reaction. On their next visit, her eyes alighted immediately on Rita's short hair.

'Her hair is her beauty!' she proclaimed and quoted from the Bible to strengthen her point. She dismissed my argument that Rita was old enough at five to take part in a decision about her hairstyle.

The next time we saw Mr and Mrs Graham, Rita's hair was still too short to plait and I made doubly sure to grease and brush it out, giving Danny similar treatment. Mrs Graham took one look at them and muttered audibly that they looked like savages. I said nothing. The overpowering influence in Danny and Rita's lives was that of the white culture with its unspoken pressures to bring them up as white children in a black skin. We were aware of the disadvantages of this approach and did our best to counteract it. Yet we did not want to take on aspects of their birth family's way of life unquestioningly. In the end, it seemed better for Rita to have plaits so that she would grow up knowing how to deal with her own hair and would look right to black people. I went back to plaiting her hair. But there was a bigger question to deal with now. We had to prepare for a court case.

11

The long road to court

Just before Easter 1981, when Rita had been with us for nearly two years and Danny for nearly a year, we started adoption proceedings. We could have applied to adopt Rita earlier, but it was fairer to Danny to adopt both children together. Danny might have felt left out, despite his desire to return to Marion, if we had made him wait. To strengthen our case, we needed to show the county court that both children were reasonably settled with us. Now it seemed the time was right to go ahead. We filled in application forms and had medical examinations prior to the county court hearing. We were anticipating that the case would be complicated only by Cynthia's refusal to agree to the adoption.

On the way to the shops one day, soon after we had filed our application with the court, Rita skipped along the road by my side.

'I'm not adopted yet, am I?'

We had hardly begun to talk about adoption with the children, but Rita must have overheard us discussing it. It was an odd coincidence that her question should come just as we were passing the county court.

'No, you're not adopted yet, but we want to adopt you.'

I tried to think of how to explain this to a three-year-old.

'It means you will be our child and stay with us until you are grown up. We shall go into the court here when we can and ask the judge if we can adopt you.'

We stopped to look at the concrete court building, its doors flanked by the lion and unicorn.

'We want to adopt Danny, too,' I went on, but Rita's attention was already elsewhere.

'Fire engine! Fire engine!' She pointed as the heavy red engine swung past. Later, when Danny was home from school, she came back to the subject of adoption.

'We are going to be adopted and stay with Mummy and Daddy forever!' Danny looked up at me. Rita's words had disturbed him.

'I know why I had to leave my mum,' he said, 'but why do I have to live with you?'

I glanced at Rita's eager face and Danny's wondering eyes. They were brother and sister, yet so different. Danny stared at me expectantly.

'Well, Danny, you went to live with Marion so she could help you find a mummy and daddy. We wanted you to live with your sister and we love you both and want to adopt you so you can belong to a family.'

'I don't want to have a sister!'

'What do you want, Danny?'

'Go back to Marion.'

'That would make us sad and Rita would be sad, too. We want to adopt you and adoption means that you will stay with us until you are grown up. You will be our son.'

'Why?'

'Because we love you and want you to stay with us.' I sat Danny on my knee. 'We will go to court and see the judge. Perhaps you can tell the judge your story.'

'I want Marion. To go back to Marion.' Danny dragged the words out.

Rita burst in. 'But that means I won't have anyone to play with!'

'Do you want to be adopted and stay with us, Rita?' I asked, knowing the answer, but wanting Danny to hear it.

'Yes!' she shouted, face alive and head nodding vigorously.

'I want to go back to Marion,' Danny said, adding, 'I want my tea now.'

While I was preparing tea, Danny watched television. Rita followed me into the kitchen with a stream of questions.

'Is Danny leaving? Why doesn't he want to stay? Why does he want Marion? Why did he live with her? How do you get adopted?'

I tried to explain that Danny's feelings were different from hers, but that he would stay with us because we were going to adopt him too. I also made a mental note to talk to Marion. Danny needed her permission to be adopted by us. He needed her to say in the simplest terms that this would be best for his future, that she was happy for him and that he could still see her when he wanted to.

One day at tea time, Danny said to me 'You aren't my real Mummy and Daddy. Cynthia and Jackson are.'

I explained again what we had told him many times before, that it was true they were his birth parents, but that we were going to adopt him. Danny stopped eating to comment.

'It's wrong for a white person to nick a brown person's children.'

I never knew where this thought had come from, but in crude terms, Danny expressed the sentiments of some of the social workers who were beginning to speak out against transracial adoption. In the early 1980s, it was no longer generally acceptable and was already becoming controversial. The alternative policy, of placing a child with a family of the same ethnicity, was being heavily promoted. Like other families who were adopting or had adopted children of a different ethnic background from their own, we saw that current opinion was critical of what we had done. It was disquieting to find ourselves on the wrong side of the argument, not only because Danny and Rita belonged to another ethnic group, but also because we sympathised with the new approach. There was nothing we could do about it. Our decisions to take Danny and Rita had been made during the early stages of the debate in this country, when thinking was rather different. We could not give them up because the policy had changed. Particularly in Rita's case, that would not have been putting their needs first, given the length of time they had been with us. We could only carry on.

The adoption process was getting slowly underway. It had taken months to prepare the various stages of the adoption application. The local authority had agreed formally that Danny and Rita were free for adoption. Sarah had crawled through thick files of papers on Cynthia and the children, extracting the information required by the court. We had all had a medical examination. Tom and I had supplied birth and marriage certificates and seen the solicitor who would handle the case should Cynthia choose to contest it. No social worker was keen to approach her, so Mrs Graham was enlisted to help. Cynthia was still visiting her regularly and Mrs Graham agreed to ask her about giving her consent to adoption. Cynthia's reply was brief: she wanted nothing to do with any adoption and would not discuss it.

When all the adoption forms were completed, the papers went to court. Danny was still saying he would tell the judge he wanted to go back to Marion. We hoped that the adoption, if it went through smoothly, would help Danny see that we wanted him.

Cynthia was to be represented in court by the Official Solicitor, who looks after the affairs of minors and others unable to conduct their own case or to give instructions. The local authority's solicitors planned to ask the county court judge at the hearing to dispense with Cynthia's consent on the grounds that she was withholding it unreasonably. Rita and even Danny were settled with us and it would be detrimental to their well-being to remove them. It was their right to be adopted, rather than to have the less secure status of foster children. Cynthia's view was that the children should never have been taken from her in the first place, but if it had to happen, then they should have gone to a black family.

The initial court date was almost immediately postponed for a week for some technical reason and then, because the Official Solicitor had not completed the necessary report, we were given yet a third date. We were told that the hearing would probably only last five minutes. Tension mounted as the days passed. All our conversations began to lead back to the court case and we wished it over. The guardian *ad litem* (now called the Children's Guardian), who is appointed by the court to represent the interests of the children, came to see us all. We discussed the adoption with both Danny and Rita, knowing that Danny was uncertain. We reassured him that he would still be able to see Marion.

One morning, Tom was opening the post as I gave the children their breakfast, when suddenly he leaped up in amazement.

'Jackson is applying for custody of the children!'

It was a week before the court hearing. Our solicitor bristled visibly when discussing this new turn of events. It seemed that Jackson had not trusted our assurance that we would let him have access to the children after the adoption. He had gone to a solicitor to discuss his rights and been told that he should definitely not limit his demands to access, but also apply for custody. This action was very much at odds with the impression he had given, both to Jennifer and us. Again, we thought Mrs Graham, encouraged by their solicitor, was behind Jackson's move. She had far more determination and sense of ownership of the children than he appeared to have.

Whatever his motive, Jackson had created a legal

nightmare for us. The hearing for the following week was abandoned while he applied for legal aid. If his request for legal aid were refused, our case would continue unchanged, except for some delay. If it were granted, a much longer delay would ensue while he applied for custody of the children. Months passed before we heard that Jackson had been granted legal aid. For a brief span of time, it looked as if there would be three court cases prior to the final adoption hearing – Jackson's application for custody, our application to adopt and a further hearing to make the children Wards of Court. We reeled back in disappointment at the delay, much more anxious now about the future.

Our solicitor came to the rescue with a plan to have all aspects of the case heard together in the High Court. We were warned that it might last three days. We would have to produce sworn affidavits, witnesses, further medical evidence and psychiatric evidence of the children's stability. The possibility of an autumn hearing moved into the spring and then the early summer with court dates set for June 1983.

We commissioned affidavits from friends, spent four hours one day briefing a barrister with our solicitor, saw the guardian *ad litem* again and had family photographs taken. Danny and Rita were becoming daily more aware of what was happening around them. Danny kept wavering about whether or not he wanted to be adopted, but he was generally against the idea. However, he was reassured by weekend visits to Marion once a term, he was happier at school and was gradually feeling more content with family life.

'Does adoption mean I can never go to tea with friends?' asked Danny one day.

'No. All it means is that you will stay with us and things will carry on just as they are now. Nothing will be any different.'

'But why won't I be allowed to go out?'

I could not help laughing.

'Staying with us doesn't mean you'll never be allowed out of the house again, Danny! It means you will grow up with us, that we will be your parents.'

I thought I managed to put his mind at rest, but when the guardian *ad litem* visited again, Danny asked the same question. Gradually we realised that in saying he did not want to be adopted, Danny was saying he did not want any changes in his life. Change was frightening. To Danny it meant moving to a new home against his will as had happened at least three times already.

'I don't know who my mummy is,' he said to me one afternoon.

'I am your mummy.'

'No you're not! It's difficult to choose. There's Marion and there's Cynthia.'

'Yes, Cynthia was your mummy when you were a baby and then Marion looked after you for a long time, but I am your mummy now.'

'I want to be adopted. Love Mummy,' said Rita, coming up and clasping me tightly.

'I love Rita. I love Danny too,' I said.

Danny squirmed and brought out a long drawn and emphatic 'No!'

'Yes, come on, of course I love you!' I said encouragingly.

'I don't love anybody. You and Marion and Cynthia should all put your money on the table and then I will choose the one with the biggest pile,' said Danny.

I laughed. 'But it's not about money – it's about having a family who love you. And you don't have to choose. The judge will decide what will happen. We hope you will stay with us and visit Marion now and then.'

There was no need for Danny to be aware that we felt some anxiety about the outcome of the case. He had enough to deal with already. He told the psychiatrist who interviewed us as a family that he did not want to be adopted. The psychiatrist took this to mean both that

Danny was frightened of change and that he was afraid to commit himself to a close relationship.

'Why don't you want to be adopted, Danny?' Tom asked at breakfast time the morning after the interview with the psychiatrist.

'I don't want to be here all the time. I don't want to be stuck with this family,' was the unvarnished reply.

'Where do you want to be, Danny?' I asked.

'I want to stay with my friends. One night in one house and then every night in a different house,' Danny replied.

'Nobody does that. All your friends live with their parents. You can stay the night with them sometimes, but you must come back to us the next day,' Tom said.

We were trying to help Danny explore the meaning of adoption without giving him the impression that he had to take responsibility for the decisions involved. But I realised we had said too much when, one day after school, Rita suddenly came up to me.

'Will I have to go away and live with someone else?' she said. Her brown eyes were staring and perturbed. For Rita to say such a thing was distressing. She could not remember any life other than with us, and her conduct gave no hint of early trauma.

Casually I answered 'No, of course not. Of course you are staying with us. The adoption is really only a piece of paper.' I decided not to discuss it again in front of her, unless she raised the subject. Months later, only ten days before the case was due to be heard in court, Rita said to me, as she was getting into the bath, 'What do you do to get adopted?'

'Oh, you ask the judge to make what is called an adoption order. It's just a piece of paper you can keep,' I said nonchalantly.

'Put on the piece of paper that I want to stay with Mummy and Daddy,' said Rita firmly. She was still thinking about the adoption case, despite our recent silence on the subject, but this was no surprise, because visits from

Sarah and the guardian *ad litem* had contrived to keep it alive in her mind.

Our barrister, so carefully briefed for our case, then announced that he was involved in another complicated case that would prevent him from attending the adoption hearing. Our solicitor asked the court for a postponement, and a date four months away, the fifth court date, was granted. We sincerely hoped that this would be the real date.

In his affidavit to the court, Jackson said that he had often asked the local authority for custody of the children and been refused, and that he had consistently tried to share the care of the baby Danny with Cynthia. We still suspected that his claim was a way of vindicating himself in the eyes of his family. A decision by the court in our favour, while he could be seen struggling to claim the children, would satisfy his conscience and give him something to say in reply to Mrs Graham. A decision in his favour, granting him full custody, would probably mean that the children would go to Mrs Graham, which we guessed was what she still wanted.

We had initially decided not to let Jackson see the children while the case was still pending. He had said nothing to us of his decision to claim custody and had allowed us to believe that he was only interested in access to the children. It seemed better to wait for the court decision and then begin afresh. Danny and Rita's memory of the one afternoon with Jackson gradually faded from their minds. We continued to see Mr and Mrs Graham every few months. Then, as the court case was postponed, it seemed unfair to the children not to let them see Jackson. Almost two years would have passed before a second meeting, had we delayed access until after the adoption. So Jackson came to our home one January afternoon in 1983, laden with a generous sack of presents. Danny and Rita remembered him. Jackson wasted no time on coming to the point.

'I know the children are happy with you and I don't expect to get custody,' he said within minutes of arrival.

I felt relieved to hear this, but neither Tom nor I followed it by asking the question it was too late to ask. Why, in that case, had he applied for custody and caused us a delay of over a year, plunging everyone into lengthy preparations leading to what promised to be a three-day drama in the High Court? We had recently learned that there would be five parties to the case, each requiring separate representation in court – the local authority, the children through the guardian *ad litem*, Cynthia, Jackson and us. Five barristers would have to be instructed and appear in turn. The answer to the unvoiced question was simple – Jackson and Mrs Graham, backed by their solicitor, were opposed to the adoption.

Again, Jackson seemed to want to talk to us about his circumstances, as much as to see the children. In the end, we had to point out that we of all people could not help him. Two months later, Jackson brought his wife, Loretta, to see Danny and Rita. Loretta chatted easily with the children and with us. There was nothing in her demeanour or conversation that suggested she was entertaining the thought of bringing up Danny and Rita. Only at the end of this visit did Jackson mention the court case. He was still expecting that we would be granted the adoption order. Loretta stood quietly at his side and did not comment. She gave the impression the matter did not concern her.

When next we saw Mr and Mrs Graham, we did not refer to the court case, but they broached the subject. They said they did not understand what Jackson was doing and did not agree with him. They wanted the children to stay with us. We thought that they were possibly keeping their path to the children open because they had reached their own conclusion about the outcome of the hearing. And it was the hearing which was now upon us.

12

The judgement

The approach of the court hearing gave rise to a flurry of
last-minute activity. Tom and I, the social workers, our
personal referees, teachers and doctors, were all busy
writing affidavits.

We were prepared to allow Jackson to visit the children
at our home or take them to see him until they were old
enough to meet him independently if they wanted to.
Cynthia's request for contact posed more of a problem.
Danny had recently said on several occasions that he
wanted to see her. Her psychiatrist reported that she
wanted to see the children every week and he suggested
that she should see them once a month. One of her social
workers said Cynthia intended to build a relationship with
the children in the hope of one day having them back. Rita
said she did not want to see Cynthia; she still remembered
the events of the last visit three years earlier. We decided to
agree to contact with Danny once a term, in a social
worker's office, with supervision, and only if her
psychiatrist felt she was well enough at the time. Rita could
join in later if she wished. Each visit would have to go well
in order for the next one to take place. The purpose of
contact would be to enable Danny to understand his past,

and have nothing to do with any idea of his going to live with Cynthia.

Jackson dropped in to see us two weeks before the court hearing. For the last three months he had been working on a house in the next street. We were pleased to see him and later that afternoon, while Danny was at a gym class, I took Rita to where Jackson was working. It turned out to be the house of a family we knew. Jackson was delighted to see Rita and a little knot of mothers gathered round to be introduced to him.

Jackson brought Loretta to see us again a week later. We had a lively conversation about almost anything but the court case, now only a week away. Loretta was pregnant, with the baby due to arrive soon. Danny and Rita were happy to see Jackson. He played with them and bounced them on his knee. He was developing an easy-going relationship with them, which we thought could be only beneficial.

Mr and Mrs Graham also came to see Danny and Rita, bringing two foster children. Mrs Graham was overjoyed to see Rita's plaits. They reiterated their support of our application to adopt.

'Will you apply to adopt your foster children?' I asked.

'Never!' replied Mrs Graham firmly. 'We are afraid of what revenge their mother's family would take. They have threatened us with a knife, so she has told us. It's all right to foster them, but to adopt them would be taking them away from their mother.'

Like Cynthia, the mother was suffering from a serious mental illness, which prevented her from having the care of her children.

'Do you think that if they were going to stay with you permanently they would have a right to be adopted?' Tom asked.

'Well, yes, we would adopt them, but we are too frightened of what would happen.'

We had the impression that Mr and Mrs Graham felt

that adoption was wrong in principle. In the Caribbean, fostering is common, but legal adoption is rare and almost seen as a form of theft. Knowing this helped us to understand Cynthia's unwavering refusal to agree to adoption.

We saw our barrister in his chambers at the Inns of Court before the court hearing. He fired off dozens of questions about our motives, about access for Jackson and Cynthia and about how we would help the children with their sense of ethnic identity. He warned us that the case would probably take four days and that we might have to be in the witness box for two hours. Tom and I were both on tenterhooks and I began to dread the day.

On the morning of the hearing, I felt relieved that the waiting was now over. We tried to explain to Danny and Rita, without creating anxiety, that we were going to court. We then took them to school and made our way to the Law Courts. Everyone involved in the case collected outside the judge's chamber. Apart from us, our barrister, his two pupils, our solicitor and her clerk, there were the guardian *ad litem*, Cynthia, Jackson, Sarah and Jennifer, the local authority's barrister, Jackson's solicitor and barrister, Cynthia's current social worker (Jennifer had been steered away from direct contact with Cynthia after she had been attacked), the Official Solicitor's representative and their barrister – a total of 18 people.

Cynthia was whisked away to a seat at the end of the corridor. I had not seen her for three years. The attractive if bizarrely dressed young woman of our earlier acquaintance looked very different. Her manner was heavy and still. The drugs, which had given her back a measure of sanity, had somehow diminished her strong presence. Jennifer went up to Cynthia and spoke to her. Cynthia apologised for what had happened when we all last met.

Jackson strolled in, looking rather more informal and nonchalant than I imagined he was feeling. He ignored Cynthia, taking care to stand where she could not see him.

He was concerned about Loretta, as the baby was due at any time.

For three hours we hovered in small constantly changing groups, waiting for the judge, who was hearing another case. The time was not wasted as our barrister conferred first with one party and then another, slowly working towards agreement on the points at issue. He persuaded Jackson to drop the case for custody, which everyone but Jackson and his solicitor knew could not be argued seriously. He worked out a declaration of intent concerning Jackson's contact with the children, which would not form part of the adoption order, but remain on the court file.

The barrister for the Official Solicitor produced a written summary of Cynthia's views. She would still not agree to the adoption and she wanted access to the children. We had already drawn up another declaration of intent with our barrister, concerning contact with Cynthia. The guardian *ad litem* agreed to act as liaison and supervise the meetings.

No contact was to take place with either parent unless we considered it in the interests of the children. We would not surrender any parental rights. The arrangements rested instead on the good faith of everyone involved.

By early afternoon the case was free of all dispute except Cynthia's refusal to consent to the adoption. The judge was still not available and Cynthia went home, asking her barrister to speak for her. It began to look as if the hearing could be discharged in one day. However, the judge, known for his inquisitorial style, might not accept the agreements reached by the barristers. The whole drama might still have to be staged, with witnesses summoned to appear in court.

Then another judge was found who was free to hear the case immediately. The moment had come.

We filed slowly into the court chamber. It was not a large room, but the judge, seated on a raised platform, seemed to look down on us from a distance. Almost his first question concerned the unusually large number of people in court. He was assured that everyone present had a right to be there.

Our barrister opened the hearing by explaining the background to the case and the agreements reached. He asked the judge to dispense with Cynthia's consent to the adoption on the grounds that she was withholding it unreasonably, to make an adoption order, to accept the declarations of intent on the court file for future reference, and to discharge the children as wards of court. They had been made wards of the High Court earlier in the proceedings as a temporary precautionary measure to prevent their removal from us. The judge asked some factual questions and retired to his chambers to read the case papers.

Everyone, except Jackson, who remained in the courtroom, waited in the corridor again. After three-quarters of an hour, we were summoned back. We immediately sensed a shift in the judge's previously severe manner.

'If there is one thing that shines out like a beacon in this case, it is the overwhelming argument in favour of an adoption order,' he said. Tom and I exchanged glances of relief. Jackson was slumped in his seat.

Cynthia's refusal to consent to the adoption had to be considered. The test applied at the time was 'what would a reasonable mother do in such circumstances?' The barrister retained by the Official Solicitor spoke for Cynthia, explaining that a refusal to consent to adoption, even when the children have been settled in their new home for years, was not uncommon, but that he could find no arguments against the making of an adoption order. He added that, despite her illness, Cynthia was perfectly capable of understanding the meaning of adoption and of making a decision about it.

The judge dispensed with Cynthia's agreement to adoption, on the grounds that it was in the interests of the children, which were paramount, to make the adoption order, and give them as much security under the law as possible. He accepted the declarations of intent, whilst noting that they were not conditions of the adoption order, and he discharged the wardship. The adoption order was made in our favour. Listening to these legal decisions, I felt surprisingly hollow.

After all the anxieties of the past few years, it was gratifying to hear the judge say that the one thing agreed by all parties was that we had offered an excellent home to Danny and Rita, which was difficult to praise too highly.

The judgement said:

> *They have taken on, particularly in the case of Danny, who was an older child when he came to them, a very difficult task, one which they have filled to date with great ability. The task has been made the more difficult in their case and they have handled the point with great sensitivity, it seems to me, in that both Danny and Rita are black, in the sense that they are children of West Indian parents and the applicants are white, and in order to deal with that possible difficulty the applicants have, in fact, encouraged access by the children to their natural parents so far as that has been possible, and indeed to remoter relations, grandparents as well. They have indicated that they are prepared to continue that practice so far as they are satisfied that it is in the welfare of the children, and declarations of intent as between themselves and the mother on the one hand and Mr Jackson Graham on the other have been entered into, and although they will not be forming part of any order that I make, I have agreed that such declarations be recorded on the court file.*

As the judgment moved on to the making of the adoption order, the judge said, 'It always gives me, at any rate, great pleasure when I can promote the welfare of children by making a positive order in this way. It is one of the nicer things that happens to a judge sitting as a judge of the Family Division.'

As I listened to the judgement, my feeling of hollowness gave way to one of lightness and joy. I smiled across at Tom, who looked similarly pleased. The judgement was that of a middle-aged white man and it came at the end of a series of events that had taken Danny and Rita from their black family several years previously but, given all that, it seemed right for the circumstances in which it was made. As we began to leave the court, our pleasure was marred by the sight of Jackson in tears. I touched his arm.

'Jackson, please ring us when the baby arrives,' I said. I meant that I wanted him to trust us about the arrangements for seeing the children. He nodded, his head in his hands, and walked away.

That night, we took Danny and Rita out for a meal to celebrate. Rita was happy about the adoption when we talked about it over the meal. Danny, still clinging to the past, was more cautious. Over the next days and weeks, family and friends congratulated us. Rita took it all in her stride, but Danny was uneasy. He stayed with Marion for a weekend and seemed to be enjoying himself, until the Sunday morning, when he broke down in tears, saying he had not wanted to be adopted.

One morning the following week, the school rang to say that Danny had been gloomy and tearful at school, not only earlier that morning, but also during the previous week. I was reminded of Jackson's mood at the end of the court hearing. The head teacher and class teacher had talked to Danny about the adoption when he showed signs of being upset. Danny told them that he had changed his mind; he did not want to be adopted. He wanted to live with Marion. He also said he had needed more time to decide. The teachers were sympathetic, but realistic in their approach. That evening, I said to Danny:

'Tell me what happened at school today.'

'Nothing,' said Danny, as usual.

'Danny, I know you were upset about the adoption because the school rang and told me.'

I explained what the teachers had said. Danny listened reluctantly.

'Danny, even if you had more time to decide, it would be too hard for you to make this big decision. The decision was made by the judge after listening to what people had to say and reading all the papers. The judge wanted to know what you thought about it, but that was completely different from asking you to decide.'

My words may have hit their mark, because Danny did not react further to the adoption order, and life for us returned to normal. We were spared from thinking about legal proceedings for a long time.

Three days after the court hearing, Loretta had a baby boy. Jackson telephoned us with the news and we went to see the new family after Loretta came home. Mr and Mrs Graham were there as well. No one talked about the court case. It had already become history.

Danny joined Rita in deciding not to see Cynthia again for the present, but the arrangements for access were ready if they wished to change their minds. They wanted to see Jackson and Mr and Mrs Graham. We looked forward to a future that would enable the children to embrace both their cultures. We knew they might encounter difficulties, but were determined to help and protect them as long as they needed us. We were entering a peaceful phase of life – the calm before the storm.

13

Our family life

For nearly seven years after the adoption, we led a stable family life, focused largely around the children. Other children came to play and we exchanged visits with family and friends. Zach almost lived with us and seemed to go home only to sleep. The year after the adoption hearing, when Danny was eight and Rita was six, I went back to work, taking a job that was more flexible than social work. We made an arrangement with a friend, Linda and her husband, David, whose two boys were the same age as Danny and Rita: once a term we took their two boys for the weekend and Linda and David reciprocated. The adults enjoyed their free time and the children loved their weekends together. Linda worked with children with special needs and was always kind and helpful to Danny.

At six, Rita began to notice her skin colour in a different way. In her early years she accepted with few questions the fact that she was a black girl with white parents. She was amused by the efforts of white people to tan in the summer, because she knew that she would always be browner, the more so when her dark skin also tanned. Then she began to say that white skin and blonde hair were better than black skin and black hair. She was surrounded by advertising that proclaimed the ideal of the blonde white woman. She lived with white people. She yearned for (and received from one of our relatives) a Sindy doll. I tried to counteract it with a number of black dolls but they were too babyish and lacked the glamour of Sindy. No black Sindy was obtainable in England, but eventually I arranged for a friend to send one over from North America. Rita was thrilled.

We had also done our best from the beginning to find books which featured children from different "races". This was not as easy as it would be now. In these small ways we tried to help Danny and Rita develop their sense of ethnicity.

Perhaps because he was older, Danny was more colour-conscious than Rita. At seven, he stopped thinking he would turn white as he grew older. A literal child, he disliked being called black, because his skin was brown, so brown he called himself.

Amongst the local families we knew was a little girl of Rita's age whose father, Jim, was an artist in his spare time. One day, when I was collecting Rita from her friend's house, he showed me a portrait of his daughter. It was fresh and colourful and I complimented him. He offered to paint Rita's portrait. Tom and I were delighted. Rita was seven-and-a-half at the time and liked the idea of a painting of herself. Jim only wanted enough money to cover materials. No sittings would be involved as Jim was planning to use photographs. We gave him a selection of pictures, and he chose one of Rita in summer clothes, smiling at the camera. I expected to hear nothing for ages, but in a few weeks, he had finished the painting.

Rita was very curious to see the picture and could hardly wait for Jim to unwrap it. A puzzled frown crossed her face as she took a first look.

'My teeth are dirty!' she said indignantly. She bared her teeth to prove the injustice of what Jim had done. Indeed, they were pure white in real life, but in the picture Jim had avoided pure white teeth. Rita saw this as an unfair criticism, particularly when Tom and I had always insisted on twice daily teeth cleaning.

'I can see what you mean,' I said, 'but look, it's just the shadow cast by your upper lip. See how white they are outside the shadow.' I pointed to where, fortunately, Jim had allowed part of Rita's teeth to shine with toothpaste brilliance.

'It's a very good painting. I can see Rita at different ages in it – now, at 17 and again at 40,' said Tom, impressed and intrigued. Jim had somehow captured the essence of Rita. The picture of her smiling face, with only a glimpse of her shoulders and dress, revealed the different tones and colours of her skin and allowed them to dominate. The effect was full of life.

We chose a gold frame to reflect the colour and strength of the picture and hung it in the sitting room, where it received much praise. We paid Jim as much as we could possibly afford and far less than his work merited, but everyone, even Rita, once she understood the treatment of her teeth, was satisfied.

Danny and Rita went to the after school club every day now. I collected them after work. Danny was keen on football and joined a local team. Once a week, I left work early to take Rita to the ballet class she had joined at the age of four. She was a good dancer and enjoyed the classes.

Rita began to be busy after school. Apart from ballet lessons, she took piano lessons. We began a tradition, which continued for years, of holding a Christmas musical event for local friends' children and their families. The children performed and it was always a lively occasion. Although she loved music and had ability, Rita hated practising. Tom was unfailingly patient in his efforts to interest her. Rita had to be coaxed at length to begin and then would not apply herself. Her lack of practice made it hard for her to progress. Danny showed no interest in music lessons and we did not push him. He had challenges enough.

Every year, Rita took the Royal Academy ballet exams and did well. However, when she was about nine, her teacher suggested she give up ballet and change to the modern dancing class, which was held on the same day. Rita was going to be too big and strong to be a ballet dancer. Fortunately Rita was happy to change and excited by the different music and dance steps of the new class. She was developing into a talented child. She seemed bright and eager at school in those early and middle primary years. She learned to write easily and liked writing letters, especially when she could type them. We had an electric typewriter at home that she could use and she would sometimes come to work with me during school holidays and type there. She loved being read to as a child and progressed easily to reading children's novels on her own.

Rita also went to drama classes for several years. She was a confident actor. The drama group staged regular performances, with parents as the audience, and Rita also acted in school plays. At eight and on her own initiative, she wrote to a children's television programme and was invited to take part in a competition, acting the part of a Town Crier. With her powerful lungs and her stage confidence, she won easily. At ten, she appeared as Scrooge in Charles Dickens' *A Christmas Carol* at school. She learned the part to perfection and I was impressed by her total lack of stage fright. We were immensely proud of her. And her mimicry of Lenny Henry, on other occasions, had us all in stitches. Rita added singing lessons to her after-school activities. She had a lovely clear singing voice and was enthusiastic for about a year, but she would not persist and so, despite our encouragement, gave up.

By the time she was ten, Rita was putting on weight through eating sweets and biscuits and other snacks whenever she could. She was too old for me to exercise sufficient control and she saw no point at all in cutting down. I tried to avoid confronting her directly, and concentrated instead on making meals at home as fresh

97

and appetising as possible.

It was not until well over two years after we first thought of the idea that we managed to arrange psychological testing for Danny, and then only through Tom's influence with a colleague at work. It was not the way it should have been done, but for Danny's sake we felt we had to arrange help somehow. We learned that his verbal reasoning was average for his age group, but his reading age at almost nine was five-and-a-half. This suggested he could catch up on reading. He was recommended for hearing tests because he was slow to respond in conversation and for a speech therapy assessment because his speech was still unclear. Tests showed his hearing was good (as we had always thought). He saw the speech therapist, who promised to see him again but never did. We did not press for this service, because Danny's speech was improving of its own accord.

I told the head teacher about the test results and made sure he saw a copy of the psychologist's report. He was not in a position to do much. Danny was already receiving help from the special needs teacher and no other resources were available unless he was made the subject of a statement of special needs, which could have taken years to arrange. We concluded that there was probably little else we could do.

As time went on, Danny did make real progress at school and in himself. His confidence and self-esteem grew steadily. He developed into a tall, slim, handsome boy. He became more popular at school and applied himself to his work. However, he still kept a distance from us at home and always seemed to prefer the company of his friends.

In their later years at primary school, tension developed between Danny and Rita. Danny became rather dismissive of his sister. He was a boy, he was older, he had somewhat different friends and different interests. Rita clearly liked Danny and seemed proud of him. But she learned to defend herself if he was mocking or critical. They began to bicker tiresomely, but probably no more than many brothers and sisters do.

During these years we made contact with several families who had adopted children from minority ethnic groups. The local authority's adoption and fostering unit brought us together from a wide area covering several counties and we met on three or four occasions at yearly intervals. We met at the unit and brought food for a shared lunch. There were toys for the children and discussion groups for the adults.

Tom and I and the children exchanged visits with two of the families we met through this group. One family had adopted two black boys from different families; the other, two dual heritage girls from different families. All families in the group were well aware of the change in policy for placing children in need of a permanent home with families of the same ethnicity. We enjoyed sharing experiences, but neither the meetings at the unit nor the social occasions could be very frequent. We lived too far away from each other and we all had busy lives. In time the contacts withered. By contrast, contact with the Graham family was to grow, with consequences we had not foreseen.

14

Growing closer

Not long after the adoption hearing, Mrs Graham rang to ask if she could see Danny and Rita. After one or two visits back and forth, with both Tom and me, Mrs Graham again asked to take the children to church.

We agreed that Ben, Mrs Graham's eldest son and more devout than Jackson, should collect Danny and Rita every possible Sunday, and either bring them home afterwards or let us know that they were ready to be collected. The main church service was three hours long, but the children had a separate service in the same building.

The first time we collected the children straight from the church. We arrived before the service was over and were welcomed by some of the members. The church was plain inside with whitewashed walls. It was full and we squeezed into the back row. People were chanting and singing in a fervent fashion.

Danny and Rita attended church in this way for about two years. We normally made sure that they looked smart with freshly pressed clothes and well oiled skin, Danny's hair brushed and Rita's plaited. One Sunday morning, we sent Danny to church in a pair of clean, patched jeans. Mrs Graham was angry and reprimanded us. Sunday best was the requirement and nothing else would do.

Sunday was the best day for visiting Tom's parents and mine, so the children went to church only when there was nothing else planned, about once every two or three weeks. They stayed for lunch with the Grahams afterwards. At first, they enjoyed all the fuss and attention, but as Danny approached ten and became more confident about his likes and dislikes, he started to protest. Rita added her voice in agreement. The children's separate service had stopped and they found the adult service boring. Years later, Rita told us that too much was different from what she was used to and she felt she did not fit. We were not prepared to insist on the children going to church, and we explained to Mrs Graham that they would not be going any more. She was not pleased because she saw church attendance as a duty, but she had no choice about accepting our decision.

We were also dismayed about comments that Rita brought home after visits to the Graham household; for example, one of Mrs Graham's adult daughters said to Rita one day that she would not want to live with white people. We tried to explain to Rita that this remark was not meant to upset her.

Some months later, when Danny was ten and Rita was eight, their uncle Ben got married. Mrs Graham invited Danny to be a page and Rita a bridesmaid. The children were keen to take part and we agreed. The wedding was planned months in advance and Tom and I were invited as well. Mrs Graham arranged for Danny to have a suit and Rita a dress made to measure. Danny had never had a suit before, let alone one made to measure, and he was very impressed with the process of fittings. Rita was entranced by her floor length dress of lace-covered pink taffeta. The day before the wedding both children were taken by the family to have their hair done professionally.

On the day of the wedding, we drove to the church and released Danny and Rita to their duties. The church was full. Ben wore a tailcoat and the bride was in white. After they exchanged vows, the newly married couple walked back down the aisle under an arch of formally dressed groomsmen.

The bride and groom left the church in a horse and carriage and were followed to the reception by dozens of cars. Tom had to leave at this point, so I carried on alone to the reception where I found myself the only white person among six hundred guests. I was placed at a table with people I did not know; the family were sitting elsewhere; I felt privileged to be invited, and did not expect to be treated as one of the family, which clearly I was not.

The room was crowded and noisy. At the table were special napkins printed with the name of the bride and groom, one of which was lovingly preserved for years by Rita. As alcohol was prohibited by the church, soft drinks were served to accompany curry goat and rice. Danny and Rita flitted about, full of excitement, occasionally coming up to me. Jackson roamed around with a video camera. Mrs Graham told me Danny had disappeared the previous day when visiting the hairdresser. There was no opportunity to question her in detail about what had happened.

Family members sat at a high table, facing the rest of us. In front of them were ranged several enormous wedding cakes which I knew Mrs Graham had made with other relatives. I was even given a big slab to take home for the children. After the meal came speeches from the bride and groom and family members on both sides. All the speeches showed a strongly held religious belief, but the bride's speech was the most striking. She spoke like a preacher with a passionate faith, referring to the devil as if he were waiting to tempt us at every turn, and to evil as a force in its own right.

The following weekend, we went to Mrs Graham's house to collect Danny from a visit. She had offered to give him a cookery lesson. Danny was showing signs of being a good cook and could already make simple meals at home.

I thanked Mrs Graham for inviting us to the wedding, but she did not want to talk about that. Instead she said accusingly, and at some length, that Danny had head lice. Tom and I stood our ground. Head lice were a constant problem at school and Rita had them more than once, but Danny had not had them since he came to us and was not infested now. I drew him over to show Mrs Graham and, sure enough, his head was quite innocent.

Mrs Graham again mentioned that Danny had wandered off on the day of the visit to the hairdresser – he had been left in the charge of one of his other relatives. Waiting at the hairdresser's was boring so he decided to go for a walk. Apparently he had been missing for two hours. Tom and I made light of it to Mrs Graham, but resolved to talk to Danny.

We took our leave of Mrs Graham as quickly as possible after what had been a heated exchange. I was disappointed that my good feeling about the wedding had been brushed aside. On the way home, we discussed what might have been the purpose of her attack. She must have felt guilty about the fact that Danny had been lost, had no doubt also been very anxious, and assumed, not realising Danny's propensity for "not telling", that we would know about the incident, and would accuse her of neglect. So it seemed that she had diverted our attention to forestall any criticism from us.

It was not long after Ben's wedding that Mrs Graham began to foster another child. The two children placed with her earlier had returned home. Her application to become the long-term foster parent of this child came before the council's adoption panel of which I was then a member, and I wrote a letter to the department supporting her. My letter outlined her strengths – her experience in bringing up seven children, and her unstinting care of Cynthia, to whom she owed no obligation. I do not think this letter was particularly influential, and in any case it was decided that the boy concerned needed a more professional residential assessment, and he was moved. Mrs Graham was aware of my letter, but did not welcome it, even though I was trying to support her against the local authority, which I felt was failing to recognise her good qualities, and which perhaps should not have turned down her original application to foster Danny and Rita.

During our visits to the Graham family we met another son, Matthew, a carpenter. We thought he could do some work replacing floorboards in our house; giving him a job would strengthen the link with the Grahams now that Danny and Rita no longer went to church. Unfortunately, it was not to be that simple. On the day we had arranged for him to start work, with all the furniture painstakingly removed to other parts of the house, he forgot to turn up. Although I refrained from saying anything to Matthew, I made no secret at home of my irritation. I was taken aback when Danny and Rita rounded on me and said I should not criticise their uncle. It was the first evidence of a real strength of feeling for their family.

Eventually Matthew arrived. He took a long time to do the job rather badly. We had to cover the floorboards with carpet rather than rugs as we had planned, because they warped and let in draughts. It all turned out to be expensive and unsatisfactory, although Danny and Rita enjoyed Matthew's presence around the house. I did not dare be critical of Matthew's work, except privately to Tom, and knew that from now on we would have to be careful about what we said to Danny and Rita about their family. We recognised that a shift had taken place: the children had taken a step towards their birth family and away from us.

At first we saw little of Jackson after the adoption. One Christmas Eve, he turned up at almost midnight, with a sack of presents. After Danny and Rita had stopped attending church, we gained the impression that Mrs Graham relied on him to keep up the relationship, because he started visiting more often and came a few times to take the children swimming. He usually stayed for a cup of tea afterwards and we all enjoyed his company. One Sunday he invited us to lunch with Loretta and their children. We had a pleasant afternoon, and after lunch Jackson showed us videos of his holidays in Jamaica. But another Sunday, when Jackson had taken the children out, he was hours late bringing them home and I made it clear we had been worried because we did not know what was happening or where the children were.

About a year after the adoption, Danny and Rita decided to see Cynthia once every six months, under the supervision of a social worker. We took the children to the social worker's office and collected them afterwards. On one occasion Cynthia walked along the road with us after the visit. She was on her way to see her mother. She spoke slowly in the high voice I remembered and expressed herself simply. This series of meetings with Cynthia did not last long, because she then used to see the children at Mrs Graham's house on Sundays after church. Even when the children stopped attending church, they visited Mrs Graham often enough for Cynthia to see them now and again. She never pressed for more opportunities.

By the age of twelve, Danny was capable of taking the bus to Mrs Graham's house on his own. He was a tall, strong-looking boy, who achieved independence on the street early because he showed he was capable of coping with it. He walked to school on his own from the age of ten and was keen not to be seen with Rita and me on the way. At eleven, he began to attend a local comprehensive school that was over a mile away and successfully negotiated first the walk and then the bike ride. It was but a short step to taking the bus for three miles to see Mrs Graham, and then another short step to finding his way to Jackson's house. At twelve and thirteen, Danny was keen to get to know his family better and we felt this was an important part of his identity. We were glad that there was no mystery, no unknown father or mother to wonder about, but a real and accessible family. At the same time, we told ourselves he needed the stability of his home with us. So there were visits to his grandparents at the weekends, and to Jackson and Loretta where he sometimes stayed overnight. They had had another son and Danny liked the thought of having brothers.

When Danny was just thirteen and Rita eleven, Cynthia wrote to us.

It has been six years now since you adopted Danny and Rita. I remember well when we went to court that day in the West End, and what my thoughts were. Then I felt that with medication I would be able to look after the children myself. But now six years later I realise that I was wrong.

My medication makes me so sleepy that it is a struggle to care for myself. I am just too sleepy to look after two children. But I am very glad that it was you and Tom that adopted them. The children are very happy with you both and Rita especially loves you very much. Whereas six years ago I did not agree to you adopting the children now I agree wholeheartedly. I am very happy that you adopted them, for the children are blissfully happy and contented with two very loving parents. If it was not for the colour of their skin, one would not know that they are adopted children. The children would not be happier if they were with me. Now that Danny has gotten over his rickets he is a healthy young teenager, who is full of life and very happy. I am very grateful to you and Tom both for taking such good care of the children and I hope you and the children will continue to have many more happy years together. I am also very grateful to you both for letting me see the children. Everyone is surprised when I tell them my children are adopted but I still see them, which shows how big hearted both of you can be. Lots of love, Cynthia.

We were touched by this generous letter because it came from the heart and was a gift freely bestowed. Cynthia's permission for us to have the children was precious. It was ironic that, not long afterwards, there was a crisis.

15

The runaway

In the summer of 1989, when she was eleven, Rita was rushed into hospital with appendicitis and operated on immediately. She was in hospital for nearly two weeks. I took virtually the whole time off work to camp by her bedside, where Mrs Graham arrived one night with Mr Graham, Jackson and other relatives. Danny had given her the news. Rita was feeling much better by then and quite able to entertain her visitors, and Mrs Graham told us stories from her childhood in Jamaica. Jackson kindly drove us home when Rita was discharged as Tom needed our car that day. Rita had lost weight and she was pleased to be slimmer, but could not resist going back to sweets and cakes. We wondered if her excessive eating was a sign of distress caused by a growing unease with her circumstances.

That summer we travelled to Valencia for a month's holiday, having exchanged our house in England with a Spanish family's flat in a holiday village. We went sightseeing in the mornings with Rita and, to her unending delight, spent the afternoons on the beach. Rita still loved swimming, and she stayed in the water for hours. She also loved the hot weather, the ice cream and the interesting drinks at the bar. We enjoyed our time with her, glad she was over her operation.

Danny too had a wonderful holiday. He was by then thirteen-and-a-half. He spent almost no time with us at all. From early in the morning until midnight, he was gone. He met a group of teenagers as soon as we arrived and merged with them as if he had known them all his life despite the language barrier. With us, he seemed sombre and reluctant, while with his new friends he was smiling and relaxed. We had mixed feelings about all this. The holiday village was a safe environment, and we were becoming used to his increasing absences at home, but on that holiday he never came out with us and never, apart from a hurried breakfast, ate with us.

We were conscious that tensions in our relationship with Danny were simmering beneath a surface calm. We treated him with kid gloves and in a deliberately light-hearted way. Danny seemed poised for a scene – we were determined not to have one in Valencia. Rita appeared to be unaffected by Danny's behaviour. It was with great relief that we left for home.

In spite of the summer tensions, the autumn was uneventful and we spent Christmas in a cottage with my older brother, Frank, and his family. Not a cross word was spoken by anyone the entire time. We ate well and walked all the excess off in the countryside. In the dark late afternoons and evenings, we played games and talked and watched television.

It was after Christmas, when he was just fourteen, that Danny ran away from home. One morning in early January, he was late leaving for school. He had been getting later and later and that morning I tried to hurry him out of the house. He resisted and Tom and I both snapped at him at once. That did it. The thin layer of normality that had covered the growing tension in our relationship with Danny, which we had nursed carefully for eighteen months to avoid a row, cracked in seconds as Danny lost his temper.

'You're not my parents! You've got no right to tell me what to do! You're nothing! Jackson is my father and the adoption is only a piece of paper!'

He tore up to the front door and slammed it shut behind him. The whole incident had lasted only minutes. Danny was out that evening when I reached home but he arrived soon afterwards, with Zach in tow. He was still in a rage and shouted angrily at me. 'I'm leaving! I'm not staying here where I don't belong!'

The boys went upstairs. Before long they were down again, Danny still shouting that he was leaving and never coming back. I could not allow him simply to walk out, so I barred his way to the front door. Danny was by then taller than me and had all the strength of an adolescent boy. I tried to persuade him to sit down so we could talk about what had happened, but Danny was past sitting and past talking. I could not bar his way for any length of time, so I retreated.

Danny's way out was clear now and he and Zach left, slamming the door behind them with an air of finality. Rita and I sank down together on the stairs. The house seemed empty and silent but somehow echoed with a sense of calamity. Rita was holding our telephone book. She looked up at me, tears streaming down her face. I was amazed by her next words.

'I must see my granny.'

She held the telephone book open at the page with Mrs Graham's number. With a sense of foreboding that defied expression, I reassured her. 'Of course you shall see your granny,' I replied and put my arms round her.

Tom was at the door by then and we explained what had happened and that Danny had gone to stay with Zach. It seemed like a good idea for him to have a cooling-off period. We rang Zach's mother the next day and discovered that Danny was planning to stay a second night. I thought it was likely that Danny would then go on to Mrs Graham, so I rang and forewarned her. She seemed surprised and was quick to judge Danny an 'ungrateful boy' and said that he should come back to us.

Everyone we spoke to in those first few days thought Danny would come back, but Tom and I knew that he never would. It was clear to us that the day of his departure was the final straw, following eighteen months when he had seemed increasingly distant from us.

Danny duly turned up at Mrs Graham's house. As he refused to return to us, we arranged for him to stay with her for a few weeks, and we paid her what seemed like a reasonable sum to cover food and other immediate needs. At the first chance, we visited the Grahams, hoping to see Danny and talk to him. He was still enraged and at the sight of me, lunged towards me. Mrs Graham pushed him back, almost as if she were swatting a fly, and Danny subsided. We told him we wanted him to come home, but he glowered and left the room. We should have left then as well, but instead we stayed rather hopelessly for an hour. We were still numbed by Danny's departure, believing and yet not believing it. We listened almost in silence as Mrs Graham unleashed a tirade of abuse on the local authority for stealing her grandchildren. It seemed like a thinly-veiled attack on us.

Even though he had recently spent so little time with us, life at home was different without Danny. We were shocked by his absence, by the emptiness of his room and by the sudden silence. In helping him to get to know his birth family, we had unwittingly prepared him for taking his life into his own hands. He had not consciously planned to leave us, and had left in a way that was deeply hurtful to us, but he had made a choice to be with his birth family.

We embarked on the desolate task of telling everyone we knew. All these conversations followed the same pattern: the listener was sure he would return, and we expressed our own increasingly firm belief that he would not. Danny no longer needed us. Our view was that he was not mature enough to talk to us and explain how he felt, so he had engineered a disagreement that would enable him to feel justified in walking out.

Rita seemed at first to blossom after Danny left. She and Danny had continued to get along badly; he still rebuffed all her attempts to be friendly. Tom and I noticed how Rita moved around the house as if it were more her own. She could do what she liked, when she liked, more often than before. She sang more and seemed happier.

We talked to Rita about Danny's departure without being critical of him. We said we wanted him to come back, but we said nothing about our certainty that he never would. Rita listened but said little in response.

Shortly after Danny left, we wrote to Jennifer explaining what had happened and asking to see a social worker. Jennifer rang straightaway to say that she could not help us because we lived outside the area she worked in now, but she was sending our letter on to our local social services office. We heard nothing after that and some weeks later wrote to the local office. Still we heard nothing.

We made several more visits to the Graham household. Danny was still angry and would not talk to us or even see us. At his request, relayed through Rita at school, we sent several of his possessions to him. Rita took them to school. She seemed pleased about this new role of envoy, as it gave her a usefulness in Danny's eyes that she had not previously enjoyed. I felt uneasy about it, because no matter how positively we represented Danny and the Graham family to Rita, she gave the impression, whilst saying little, that she was taking sides in a dispute and that the side she had chosen to support was that of her brother.

Gradually Rita withdrew more and more into herself. Just as we had with Danny, Tom and I felt we were skating on very thin ice in our dealings with her. I suggested to Rita that she might like to move into a larger bedroom which we were using as a sort of family room and spare room. She was twelve years old by then and still occupying the little room of her early childhood. We thought she would enjoy more space and some new furniture. She showed not the slightest glimmer of interest in this plan, so we dropped it. Increasingly we felt as if we could not get through to her. We did not know it, but worse was to come.

16

In Danny's footsteps

Rita started to say that she wanted to see Mrs Graham every week. Tom and I thought this was too often and suggested she continue seeing her about once a month. Rita said nothing, not even troubling to argue her case. She may have felt some satisfaction at the restriction we imposed, as it gave her something to rebel against.

There were many small disputes, characterised by Rita's reluctance to communicate and by flashes of her temper. Her view of this period is different from mine: she remembers still being entirely happy with us.

I felt anger, combined with fear, feelings I pushed away and did not even mention to Tom. Whenever there was an argument, I made myself bite my tongue. I knew the ground was shifting beneath my feet but, apart from keeping a surface calm, I did not know what to do. Rita seemed either so remote or so angry with us that I felt powerless to get anywhere with her.

A week or two later, on a Sunday afternoon, Rita was watching television. Almost for something to say, I asked if she would like to go swimming. She refused. I stood there irresolutely. Rita turned to me and asked me what I was staring at, running her words together with an intonation borrowed from Jackson. Startled by her tone, I sent her to her room. She moved towards the door as I sank into a chair, telling myself to say nothing more. Rita turned towards me and made a dismissive sound.

I lost my temper. All the force of feeling, so suppressed over the last few weeks, overwhelmed me and I leapt up, slapping her nearest arm and leg and shouting that if she could not be friendlier, and if we could not get along better, then I knew it would all end with her running away to her grandmother, just like Danny. My worst fear, not even admitted to myself before, was out. Rita started to cry and Tom came to see what was going on. He was quite rightly angry with me for mishandling the situation. Feeling wretched, I apologised and tried to explain how I felt. Rita would not talk to me but she calmed down. Later that evening she came and put her arms around me. We had supper in a strained silence, all of us at the mercy of huge feelings.

The next day, I came home late from work to find Tom looking worried because Rita had not arrived home until 6.30. That night we wrote again to the Social Services Department about Danny. Rita seemed to spend a long time on the phone, talking to a friend.

Breakfast next morning was quiet. As Rita left for school, Tom made fun of the weight of her school bag, holding it up and joking about what she might have in there. It certainly looked more tightly packed than usual. Rita made no reply, but kissed us both goodbye and was gone.

That evening, I was home at my normal time. There was no sign of Rita. Now she was in her first year of secondary school, it was her practice to come home from school and watch television until we arrived. At 6.30 Tom came home. We were puzzling over where Rita might be, thinking she was visiting a friend and had forgotten the time, when the phone rang. Tom answered. It was Rita. I heard him gasp and tell her to come home straightaway and then that he was going to fetch her.

He put the phone down. 'It's Rita. She's at her grandmother's. She says she's left us and she's not coming back.'

Almost without a word, we scrambled into the car and drove impatiently through the rush hour traffic. We found Danny and Rita with their grandparents and other family members. The constellation was different now and it was almost as if the many years that Danny and Rita had lived with us had never happened. We were not asked to sit down but stood awkwardly in the room. The atmosphere was awful.

Rita spoke. 'You can't take me away from my granny! You told me to leave home!'

She was sitting next to Mrs Graham, clinging onto her and almost crying. I knew I should not have lost my temper, but I had never even thought of telling her to leave. She had taken the expression of my fear and twisted it into the very opposite of what I had meant.

Danny hovered, snarling.

'Rita's my sister. You've got no right to take her.' This was from Danny, who had ignored or bickered with Rita routinely in recent years, never wanting her to be with him. I permitted myself the wry thought that at last he was fighting her corner.

It emerged that Rita had secretly visited Mrs Graham the previous day after school and told her about her argument with me. Mrs Graham's immediate response had been to invite Rita to come to her, without telling us. Rita had packed enough clothes to fill her schoolbag without arousing suspicion, so Tom's joking comment must have caused her an anxious moment. Unable to keep her plans a secret, she had telephoned a friend the night before.

Mrs Graham made no effort now to pretend she accepted the adoption of Danny and Rita. She had won her grandchildren over to her side. When we said we could call the police if Rita refused to come home with us, Mrs

Graham rounded on us and threatened that the whole community would rise against us, that she would go to the papers, to court, that we could never have Danny and Rita back.

Tom and I knew we had lost. We could not persuade Rita to come with us, nor could we simply pick her up and leave. She was too big for that, and to attempt it would undoubtedly have led to the fight Danny clearly wanted. All we had on our side was the law, which at that moment seemed completely irrelevant. In silence, we drove home alone. It was just as well that we did not foresee the depths we were now to reach.

17

In the depths

I stayed awake the whole of that night and even Tom, normally a sound sleeper, hardly slept. My body felt as stiff as a board, my mind was bulging with the horror, the unreason of what had happened. Tearlessly I thought over the events of the last few days until dawn came, and then until it was time to get up.

Tom and I wrote letters to Rita and rang several times but she scarcely wanted to talk to us. I felt so guilty about the loss of the children that I thought either my body or my mind would explode. There was a moment when Tom and I hovered between turning to each other and turning on each other, but fortunately we chose the former path. Tom was deeply upset, and for weeks I was overtaken by fits of crying that would last for hours. I forced myself to go to work and found some relief there.

Family, friends and colleagues were sympathetic and did their best to console us. We struggled wearily through the days, weeks and months that followed. We had been shocked when Danny left, but this was worse. Rita was only twelve and had been with us from a much younger age than Danny. Never in my life have I yearned for anything so much as I did for Rita to come home.

For at least a year, we were in a state of shock, or recovering from it. It took two or three years for life to seem ordinary again. The combination of loss and rejection had the impact of an illness on Tom and me. We were sleepless, preoccupied and tearful, raw with emotion and unable to believe the pain would ever go. The children we had brought up and had loved as if they were our own, for eleven years, would have nothing to do with us. They could not know how we felt, because they were too young and too bound up in their own newly discovered world. For the time being, possibly forever, they had finished with us and we had no real choice but to accept their decision.

The irony of the situation was that we had the law on our side, but it would have been unthinkable to call the police. Nor did we kidnap Rita after school and bring her home as one or two friends suggested we should. It would have been a bizarre and futile contest. Had the police returned Rita, she would have taken the next bus back to the Grahams. Had we reported Mrs Graham for harbouring a minor, the resulting court case would very likely have ended in a judgment in her favour. Media and professional opinion could well have supported Rita's case for staying with her birth father's family.

One day, a few weeks after Rita had gone, Tom looked up at her portrait. It still hung where we had placed it five years previously. Her seven-year-old face smiled down at us now.

'I can't stand having this here any more,' said Tom, reaching out and swiftly unhooking the picture. He hid it in the cellar, where it could not even catch our eyes by chance.

We knew the only hope of any future relationship with Rita lay in persuasion. We wrote to her so she could see we were not angry and that we still loved her, just as we had written to Danny after he left. It was strange to be writing to the children we had been living with.

Three weeks after leaving us, Rita went on a school trip

to France, for which we had already paid. We took her clothes for the holiday to the Grahams' house. Rita did not seem to be there, and was presumably keeping, or being kept, out of our way. The following week, when Tom was working at home, Rita telephoned from France one afternoon. She was excited.

'Hello, Dad. It's Rita,' she said and chatted as if she had never left home. We felt pathetically grateful to have heard from her. She then wrote to us, using our first names, though she had always called us Mum and Dad.

> *'Hello, I'm haveing a wonderful time in France as you know from my phone call. School is OK. I'm fine, Danny is fine. I've had my hair cut propaly and have got lots of clothes. I go to Church every Sunday twice and I like it and even if i didn't have to go I'd go anyway. Yes I am going on a summer holliday (shoking isn't it)*
>
> *from Rita.*
>
> *P.S. Please can I have my camera.'*

At the beginning of May, after a delay of four months, Social Services responded to our letters. It turned out that our first letter had been shunted from one local office to another, with no one thinking to contact us, while it was decided which office should deal with it: the one in whose area we lived, the one in whose area Danny lived, or the adoption unit. In the end, the children were allocated a social worker. We thought both Danny and Rita needed help to sort out their feelings and their allegiances. For Mrs Graham, the social worker, Christine, was one of a hated species, despite being black. From what we could gather, Danny had absorbed this view; he refused to see Christine, but Rita had a few interviews with her.

Mrs Graham expected us to pay her for looking after

Rita. She had enticed Rita to run away from home and we considered that it was too much to ask us for money in the circumstances. During one conversation on the phone, she said tactlessly that the children were behaving as if they had been let out of prison. She kept ringing to ask for money. I could not stand it and one day I shouted down the phone that she should send them home instead. She did not ring again.

We sent presents to Danny and Rita on our return from a week in Morocco at the end of May, a holiday we had booked with Rita in mind and which we now undertook alone. After talking further to Christine, we wrote again to Danny and separately to Rita. Rita and Danny rang up one evening about three weeks later. Rita said she wanted to go to Jamaica and America in the summer and that Jackson had promised to take her. It was an edgy conversation. I tried to keep it light but, in doing so, found it hard to know what to say. Danny came on the phone and kept asking us to change his name. I said it was up to him if he wanted to use Jackson's surname. He seemed not to understand me, because he threatened me, something he had done on the phone before. I hung up.

Tom and I felt that the phone call needed to be followed up, so we wrote to Danny to say that it was up to him if he wanted to use the name Graham, but that to help him, we had written to his year tutor so his name could be changed at school. We also told him not to threaten us again. We signed the letter with our first names, implicitly acknowledging the changed relationship.

At the same time as writing to Danny, we wrote again to Rita, asking her to come and see us. We wrote also to the Department of Social Security giving our permission for child benefit and income support concerning the children to be paid to Mrs Graham. Tom and I were upset to think of our children, who had never wanted for anything in all their time with us, living on state benefits. At the same time, we knew Mrs Graham would expect Jackson to contribute. He had often seemed to be plentifully supplied with cash.

Danny and Rita seemed far away. Yet events were to show that they had not disappeared.

18

Letters arrive

Three days after writing to Rita, we came home to find her sitting on our doorstep with her new friend Molly. It was the end of June. Even in the weeks since she had left us, she seemed to have grown taller. Her hair, despite Mrs Graham's fierce view that it should never be cut, was short. It looked pretty. It was a hot day in June, but Rita was dressed in thick jeans and a woollen jumper, despite the claim in her letter of having new clothes.

'You told me to come and see you,' she said defensively, after we greeted her. We invited the girls in. Rita had a box of chocolates and handed them round. She wanted to know why we had said that her grandmother had betrayed us. We could not remember using that word and simply said that it must have been a remark made in the heat of the moment. We felt betrayed, but, desperate to keep the channels of communication open with Rita, we thought we had not said so.

Rita went upstairs to see her room, which was untouched since her departure, and tried on some of her clothes. She and Molly ran around the house, giggling with excitement. As the girls left, I watched Rita walk away. She did not look back. Later that evening Molly's mother rang to say that Molly thought that Rita might come back to us. I knew she would not, and that her visit had been a kind of farewell. Molly's mother went on to say that she had invited Rita to visit Molly, but Jackson had been unfriendly on the phone.

The grapevine gave us some information about Danny but told us little about Rita, because she did not keep up with her old friends. Only Molly's mother had any contact with her. Rita seemed to have much less freedom to go out than Danny. She was expected to go home after school and to look after the little children of her aunts and uncles. It appeared she was discouraged from visiting her white friends, and spent all her free time either in caring for her grandparents or the children. We felt that Rita was being used to serve the needs of others, rather than allowed to enjoy the remaining time of her childhood and concentrate on her studies. But it might have felt very different to her. From what we gathered, there was a great deal of rejoicing in the family about the advent of Danny and Rita. Soon even the scant news of Rita from the one source dried up. Rita either refused to see Molly any more or was not allowed to.

We had already visited the school to see Rita's tutor about her leaving home. We went again on Open Day at the end of the summer term. Hearing that Rita and her grandmother were expected later that same evening, we read Rita's report and handed it back. The message throughout the report was that she was underachieving.

After this visit to the school, I wrote to Rita explaining our holiday plans for the summer. Going away without Danny and Rita was an enormous step to take. I felt as if we were deserting them, as if somehow I should stay at home and wait in case they suddenly turned up. But I knew in my heart that such a course of action would have been futile.

Before going on holiday, we received a letter from the solicitor who had represented the local authority in the adoption case, enclosing another from the solicitor who had represented Jackson and was now writing on Mrs Graham's behalf. The enclosed letter retold the events of the past few months from Mrs Graham's point of view, as if we had rejected both Danny and Rita. It asked if we would agree to Danny and Rita being received into care and placed with Mrs Graham as her foster children. The motive appeared to be financial. We replied that such a move would be premature, particularly in Rita's case, as we were hoping for her return. We were not prepared to take any action that would make it seem as if we were giving up Danny and Rita. We said that we understood there were financial difficulties, but that we did not think it was reasonable to be expected to give up our children to resolve them.

Returning from our summer holiday, we found a second letter from Rita.

> 'I recived you're note and read it with intrest. It was intresting to see how you refuse to let go of me. although I blame a fraction of that on [my teacher] for giving you a copy of my report. I fail to see what this has got to do with you at all........No, I won't be comming to see you. I understand I'm correct in saying you've allowed Danny to be called Graham at school I think that is only jus scince that is his name. I cant come to terms with why you cant let us have our names. You have yours everyone else has theres I don't see why we can't have ours. further more thats the only things I want from you apart from another (sob) story letter. I would apreciate it if you stopped writting to me for I don't wish to hear from you again. From Rita Graham.'

We were upset to receive this letter, even though it was written by a child who could not possibly be expected to understand how we felt. And we had not refused to let Rita use her grandparents' name. She had been misinformed. Despite Rita's request, we felt we had to write back so that she should not feel rejected. We gave our letter to Christine, and received a note from her saying that Rita refused to accept our letter and did not want any contact with us at present. We began to feel we had done enough to show Rita we had not rejected her. It was time to take a step back.

Christine wrote again, enclosing a letter dictated by Danny. It was addressed to both of us, although in parts it appeared to be meant only for me.

> 'I am writing to apologise and to thank you because I did leave in a rather bad way, but you got in the way when I asked politely for you to get out of my way.
>
> I am writing to say thank you for all the places and the countries you took me to even though I did not enjoy sightseeing. I enjoyed the visits. Thank you for taking me to Valencia and all the other holidays. Thank you for the leather purse from Morocco. I know that in some ways I have behaved badly. Now I realise that I should see it from your point of view and I do. I realise that when you adopt someone you take a big chance if they have relatives to go to. It would have been safer to adopt an orphan with no family to go to. You may think I have been mean or out of order, but if you are not getting on with someone it is only right to do something about it. In the eight months of being with my family, I realise how much I have missed out on. Sometimes I wonder how it would have been if I had lived with (there followed a sentence that Christine had crossed out). I have also learned a lot that I should have learned. In one way it is good for me that it has turned out this way, otherwise I would not have learned about God and other things. You should, if you have not already, try to see it from my point of view. We believe that God wanted it to go this way otherwise I would not be where I am as a Christian. It is good I came here

because when I think about what kind of person I would have become because i had become an unco-operative child, I think I would have got worse. You did what you thought was the right way to bring me up. Lots of people bring up their kids in different ways. When Granny says that you could not bring us up properly, it does not mean that you are a bad mother, it is just that the way you think and do things is not right. When I was really young and had eczema you did not have time to put cream on it. Granny believes if you cared you would have had time, that is why Granny doubts you as a mother.

Jamaicans they protect their children and are really strict. Jamaicans and English are very different and very similar, it is very confusing. You gave me lots of choice and freedom. Gran is Jamaican and does not see this as right.

I know you may say Danny is not old enough to change his name, because you are still hurting, but remember you took the risk of taking me in and I did not ask to be taken in. So, you should not try to annoy me or get me back. If you had not come along, the Grahams would have found me. Anyway, I am rather happy it has turned out okay and sorry about the bad things. You gave me lots of choice to travel. Jamaicans only go to America and Jamaica. I liked you introducing me to your friends and all the other nice things. I am sorry if I upset you but it is the way it goes. The Grahams say that I should have just left but I know that you would not have let me go if I had not caused any trouble. Still, it could have been worse and it is all over now. One thing I have learned from knowing about God is not to worry and let things get you down. You may think it is rubbish I want to talk about God. I hope you appreciate this letter. I will not be hurt. I am sorry for everything.

> *P.S. Please note what I said about the changing of my name.'*

Danny had forgotten how I creamed his skin every night after his bath for years until he learned to do it himself, how I took him numerous times to the doctor about his eczema and a whole range of other problems. Nor had we refused him a change of name. His grandmother was trying to undermine our influence in Danny's life. It was unfair, but there was nothing we could do about it. Danny would have to make up his own mind about his childhood.

These misconceptions apart, this letter from a boy of fourteen who had left us in a terrible rage only months before was thoughtful and mature. It was honest and appreciative. It showed an ability to try to see things from our point of view, tried to define some of the differences between the two cultures in his life, and told us about his new religious faith. It also confirmed that he was never coming back. We heard nothing more from Danny or about him for some months.

For Hallowe'en, which we had always celebrated with a party and dressing up, I confined myself to sending Rita some funny masks and novelties with a little card that simply sent our love.

In November 1990, seven months after Rita had left, we were asked to see the local authority's solicitor as Christine was worried that Rita was depressed and there was a question about whether the department should apply for wardship of the children. We doubted that court action would be effective. We wanted Rita back and we recognised that Danny had moved on. We were keeping the door open for the children should they need us. Yet it was not easy to decide what to do. We had a nagging feeling that Rita might want a decision made for her and would perhaps accept, inwardly as well as outwardly, being told to come home. In the end, after discussion with the solicitor, we took no action ourselves and nor did the local authority at that point. On balance, it seemed unlikely that Rita wanted to return to us and also unlikely that a court would order a black child of nearly thirteen to return to white adoptive parents against her will.

The solicitor told us how shocked she had been to hear of the children's departure and how the news had resounded through the adoption unit where we had been regarded as a successful adoptive family.

Rita was not in touch with us, but Danny had made important progress. We began to feel hope.

19

Danny in touch

We continued to hear news of Danny through the local grapevine. The parents of the friends he visited did not like to question him too much, but we were keen to grasp even a few crumbs of information. This was a source of comfort as it helped us feel that Danny had not altogether disappeared.

Nearly a year after he had left home, when Danny was not quite fifteen, he visited our friend Linda. He told her he was no longer angry with us and would come and see us soon. He felt that he had done a lot of thinking since he left and he appreciated that we had taught him to stand up for himself and to think and speak for himself. He had good memories of his life with us – the holidays, friends and outings. He had thought he was the cause of differences between us and felt he was a burden to us. He did not realise all families sometimes have arguments, but had quickly learned from his grandparents that they did. But he said that he and Rita stood up to their grandmother and did not simply obey her. For her part, she apparently complained that she should not be expected to change.

Danny also told Linda that he worked in a restaurant in the evenings after school and at weekends and had earned well in the summer. He had been given a great deal of advice by his birth family, but did not think that anyone listened to how *he* felt. He liked their religion. Linda got the impression that he was busy with his own life and had little time for Rita. He told her that Rita was not allowed out in the dark and that she swore a lot and was grumpy.

A few months later, Danny wrote to my younger brother, Richard, and his family in reply to a letter from them. We saw the letter, which impressed and encouraged us. It showed a boy who was well adjusted to his new circumstances and leading a full and interesting life. He obviously had to work hard to earn money. But there was not a single complaint and he was thoughtful enough to remember and ask after everyone. Thinking of the sick and malnourished baby who had been taken from Cynthia, and the confused and unhappy little boy who had first come to us, I felt he had made enormous progress.

With no warning, but true to what he had said to Linda, Danny came to see us. Fifteen months had passed since his departure. It was on an evening when I was at home sorting through some books in what had been Rita's bedroom. I had eventually redecorated it and made it into a study. It was April 1991. On hearing a knock at the door, I opened it to see Danny. Aged fifteen, he was now taller than ever and smartly dressed.

'I've come to see how you are,' he said.

I was so happy and invited him in. It was such a shame that Tom was out. Danny said he appreciated what we had done for him and he particularly remembered the holidays he had enjoyed with us. He talked about school – he was working towards his GCSE exams. Neither of us mentioned his grandmother, but I assumed that he would keep his visit to us a secret. He spent most of the time talking about his conversion to the Church of God. He said little about Rita, only that she watched a lot of television, stayed up late at night and was bad-tempered.

Danny had matured since we last saw him. He had

stopped hating us and could say what he had liked about living with us. He was able to make this gesture of bridge-building, from which many adults would have fled. He seemed so sensible and yet I could not help wondering whether it was his lack of attachment to us that enabled him to behave so well. I encouraged Danny to come and see us again and we parted on good terms.

Months went by in which we heard nothing of or from Danny and Rita. Then, nearly two years after Rita had left us, the local authority rang. The school had contacted them. It seemed that Rita was getting along badly at home, where she was angry and difficult. Jackson had threatened to come up to the school and beat her in front of everyone. The school was also worried because she was so moody.

Tom and I were not surprised at this news. Although we began to wonder whether Rita would come back to us, we knew that it was too much of a hope and too little of a real prospect.

Then Jackson wrote, asking to see us about the children. We had heard he had left Loretta, but we were not sure of his whereabouts. In the absence of an address or phone number on his letter, we wrote back both to his home and to Mrs Graham's address, asking him to ring and arrange a time. There was no reply to either of my letters and we never heard from him again.

The local authority decided to go to court because Mrs Graham was refusing them access to Rita. In January 1992, the Juvenile Court appointed a guardian *ad litem* to act in the interests of the child. We were served a copy of the order, but otherwise not involved. Tom and I said we would of course have Rita back. Tom had thought for some time that an incident might result in a rift between Rita and her family that would make her want to return to us. I was less sure. There had been something final about Rita's departure and complete refusal to have anything to do with us that made me doubt seriously that she would turn to us even if in need. The guardian *ad litem* recommended that

Mrs Graham go to court to obtain a Residence Order under the 1989 Children Act. This would give her a legal right to have the children living with her. She needed no persuading. The Residence Order could not supersede the adoption in law and to us seemed pointless, but it was clearly something Mrs Graham wanted.

We turned again to the local authority solicitor, not with any hope of persuading the children to return, but because we doubted that a Residence Order was appropriate. We had already given our tacit consent to the children living with their grandparents. We were concerned also that the court might require us to make maintenance payments to Mrs Graham, so that she would not have to claim Income Support for the children. And we were worried that Mrs Graham could use the order to take the children abroad without consulting us. Having heard rumours that she and her husband planned to retire to Jamaica and take the children with them, we wanted to be sure of our rights. The solicitor agreed to represent us and in September 1992, well over two years after they had run away, Danny and Rita were made the subjects of Residence Orders. We were spared having to attend court or make any maintenance payments.

Naturally this court case, which dragged on for six months, awoke bruised feelings which had scarcely had time to subside. When it was over, the solicitor wrote us a consoling letter explaining that the judge had been very sympathetic and had expressed the hope that the children would want to see us in future.

We sent the children birthday and Christmas cards, with money enclosed, but made no other attempts to contact them. Then, after Christmas, Danny dropped in to see us one evening. We were so pleased to see him, especially as Tom had not seen Danny since he had left home three years before. He told us about school and his Saturday job. He seemed relaxed and friendly. It was not long before we were showing him photographs of his childhood, which he took great delight in. He tried, unsuccessfully, to convert us to his religion. I gave him some money for his birthday.

Still there was no word from Rita. Then unexpectedly, soon after Danny's visit, when she was just fifteen, Rita sent us a belated Christmas card. 'Thank you very much for my birthday card. I hope you have a wonderfull christmas. Love, Rita.'

It was the first time Rita had been in touch for over two years. The friendly tone suggested she no longer felt angry with us. We could not help hoping that we would hear from her again.

A year later, in the autumn of 1993, when Danny was nearly eighteen and Rita nearly sixteen, Mrs Graham went to court again. Mr Graham had died and Danny and Rita were living with only their grandmother and an uncle.

This time the court was asked to change their surname – just in time because the papers were headed 'Application to Change the Surname of a Child' and the case was to be heard only a week before Danny's eighteenth birthday. The court papers were full of errors. Mrs Graham claimed the children wanted to have their former name and had gone back to live with her. In fact, they had never had her family name and had never lived with her before. From birth until the adoption they had used Cynthia's surname. The papers revealed several other inaccuracies. I felt angry at the way Mrs Graham kept rubbing salt into our wounds by going to court. This was the second court case she had instigated since the children had left and both had stirred up our feelings, brought back sadness, and achieved nothing from our point of view.

On the way home from work one November evening, nearly four years after Danny had left home, my attention was drawn to a group of boys just ahead. It was dark and I was nearly at the corner of our street. My hurried walk meant I soon caught up with them. I recognised Zach, much grown since I had seen him last. As I drew closer, a boy detached himself slightly from the group and looked round. It was Danny. I had not seen him for nearly a year, and he had grown even taller. Seeing me, the other boys stood aside. Danny smiled down from his surprising height. Standing in the cold air, we exchanged brief snippets of news: Danny was at college, in the first term of a course in business studies. He did not mention Rita until I asked about her, when he said briefly that she was all right. He seemed calm and at ease with himself. He was going to the cinema with his friends so there was no time for him to come in and see Tom. I was so pleased to have seen him.

On a subsequent visit to Linda, Danny said Rita was taking her exams in the summer and that she was working hard for them. He said that she wanted to do well and realised that it was her only way to escape. Hearing of this conversation, Tom and I could not help noticing the expression Danny had used. Had Rita gone from idealising her family to wanting to escape from them, or at least to wanting an escape from a future of domestic ties and low aspirations?

Danny continued to see us after this chance encounter on the street corner. Arriving late one evening in the hope of catching us in, he seemed well and chatted easily. He was starting to think that the course in business studies was too much of a struggle and that he would do better to try learning a trade. He mentioned nothing about his religious activities until curiosity overcame me. We learned he was no longer attending the full array of religious meetings in which he had previously taken part. He said Rita was working for her GCSEs and had applied to do a course in business studies.

Tom then saw Danny in a local supermarket where he was working as a cashier to support his second year in college. Danny asked if he could visit after his shift, which he did. Unfortunately, I was out, but Tom reported that Danny had moved from Mrs Graham's house and was staying in a flat with another young man. He was enjoying the independence, but having to support himself unaided. They looked at pictures of our holiday with Linda and her family and other friends. Danny showed not a hint of envy. When Tom asked after Rita, as we always did, he said she had missed some of her GCSE exams.

Danny dropped in again one Friday evening just after the following Christmas. Tom and I were cooking supper and Danny sat and watched us while we talked. He stayed for an hour that flew past.

'I was just passing by on my way to a party and I thought I would see if you were here.' Danny followed me into the kitchen. He seemed to be getting taller and taller until he subsided into a chair.

'I'm into my second year at college now but I'm thinking of becoming an apprentice mechanic – a trade would suit me better. I don't think I really want a pen and paper job after all.'

'That would be a very useful skill to have,' said Tom. 'Can the college help you find a job where you can learn the trade?'

'Yes, well, I'm looking into it,' said Danny. 'It's all right at the moment. Lots of my friends go to the same college and we have a good time. We go to nightclubs. You've got to have money now. Everyone at college is very smart and it really matters what you wear. I mean the label matters.'

We looked at what seemed to be brand new trainers on Danny's feet. He was always well dressed.

'Are you still working at the supermarket?' asked Tom.

'No, I've given all that up now, because college takes all day and it's a long journey every morning. So I've just got my grant, but I don't pay any rent, because I'm just staying at the flat. I'll be moving out soon. I've put in for a council flat,' said Danny easily.

Tom and I were surprised, as council flats were hard enough to obtain for a family with children, let alone for a single young man. We tried to warn Danny, but he looked at us with amusement as if we were fussing unnecessarily.

'I've got a girlfriend now,' Danny said, looking very pleased. 'We go out to parties at weekends.'

'What about church at weekends?' asked Tom.

Danny explained that he still believed in God but no longer went to church.

'What does your granny say to that?' said Tom, mischievously. Danny launched into an affectionate parody of Mrs Graham, which conveyed that she thought she had done her best to save his soul but it was now up to him.

Then Danny started to talk about Jackson's youngest son, his half-brother, now aged six. He was angry because the little boy had been sent away to Jamaica, to be brought up by relatives. It appeared that Loretta was finding him too difficult. Danny was feeling the loss. I asked whether Danny had seen Marion. I had earlier given him her phone number.

'No, I'm waiting until I've got a car,' said Danny.

'Why not go on the train?' Tom asked.

Danny was unimpressed.

'No, I want to drive up in my car, so she can see I'm a success,' he said. 'I've taken some driving lessons and I want to take my test when I can.'

'It's a good idea to take your test,' I said. I thought of adding that Marion would not care whether Danny had a car or not, but it was clear that Danny cared, so I stayed silent.

As Danny left, I gave him some money for his birthday, which he accepted with glee, because he wanted to take his girlfriend out. Tom said goodbye, hoping we would see Danny again soon, and I followed him out to the street to look at his new bike. There were no lights on the bike and it was night-time. I could not resist saying something about the need for bicycle lights at night, but Danny dismissed my comment airily. It was different where he lived. No one had bicycle lights. He rode off along the pavement and disappeared into the evening dark. I wondered how many months it would be before we would see him again, but not whether we would see him.

In fact, it was not long before his next visit. He came round to ask if we would help him open a bank account. He wanted to use our address and open the account in our surname. I thought back to all the preoccupation with changing the children's names to Graham as I agreed to Danny's request. He could not use his own address, as he was not the tenant, and it seemed pointless to put difficulties in his way.

Danny continued to keep in spasmodic contact with us, although he would not give us his address, because he said he could not receive any mail. He had to work hard keeping in touch with everyone, as no one could contact him, but he did not mind. He seemed generally buoyant about life, hard working and good-humoured.

Hearing from Rita allowed us to hope that we might see her. But it had to be her idea. We did not want her to feel that she had to bend to our wishes.

20

Rita makes a move

Nearly five years elapsed after her visit with Molly before we saw Rita again. Then one autumn day, when Tom was working at home, the telephone rang. It was Rita. Tom was astonished.

'I meant to ring ages ago but I kept putting it off because I was nervous...I didn't take any of my exams and I've left school now...I'm a student at college and I'm taking a GNVQ in business studies. I've got to get myself together, I don't think I've been very together lately.'

'What about coming to see us? We'd love to see you.'

'I want to, but it's difficult. After college I have to go home and cook every evening.'

'Come at the weekend then.'

'Well, I'll think about it and give you a call.'

For a week we heard nothing. Then, early one evening, Rita rang to say she would come and see us. On the chosen day, I felt so nervous that I cleaned the house, and even made my way through a pile of ironing. The prospect of seeing Rita was extraordinary. Tom and I agreed we would strike a positive note; we would not mention the fact that Rita had not taken her GCSEs; we would not talk about Mrs Graham unless she came up in the conversation; we would avoid any comparisons of Rita's old life and her current one.

The agreed time of three o'clock came and went as I ironed away. It was pouring with rain and no doubt the buses were running late. At half past three, just as I was beginning to think Rita was not coming after all, there was a loud knock on the front door, and there she was.

As I kissed the tall young woman who was standing before us, I was suddenly aware that I was assuming a familiarity that Rita might not feel. She was recognisable, but she had changed a great deal. She had grown from a child of twelve into a woman of nearly seventeen. She was as tall as Tom. Her hair was pulled back into a bun and she was plainly but neatly dressed. We all sat down, no doubt all of us feeling nervous, and talked about her bus journey and how the weather was spoiling the chances of a good Guy Fawkes night.

I disappeared into the kitchen to make the tea and came back to hear Rita talking about the course in business studies she was taking at a local college. It was the beginner's level GNVQ, and many of the students were from overseas. She was finding it too easy, and there was a plan to move her to an intermediate group. One of her old school friends was on the course with her, and she had made a new friend as well. She had a grant to pay her college fees, but was otherwise presumably still dependent on Income Support. We refrained from asking what might have seemed intrusive questions about money. Rita spent four days a week at college, but did not have a part-time job. The remainder of her time was taken up with housework and seeing friends and relatives.

School had evidently not been a success. She had become bored, for reasons it seemed better not to explore at that point. Her attendance had not been good – she had been late in the mornings and she revealed that Sky television had sometimes 'kept me up until 5am watching films'. I remembered the bright eleven-year-old who had left primary school in the top band of the ability range. But I also remembered her lack of application to schoolwork in her last year with us. Were her problems at school a direct result of leaving us? School might have seemed less relevant in her birth family. Yet Danny's departure from us did not seem to have had an adverse effect on his education, and in the end he, the boy who had disliked "hard work", had done well, given his earlier problems. But he was a boy and had a lot more freedom now than Rita.

We exchanged news of the people we all knew: friends and relatives, teachers and other acquaintances. Rita saw quite a lot of Cynthia, who had not needed to go back into hospital for many years. We knew Jackson had moved further away with Loretta and their children and had eventually left them. Rita referred to Cynthia and Jackson as mum and dad. Even after five years it sounded strange to me.

When the conversation faltered, Tom asked Rita if she would like a look around the house.

Rita jumped up with alacrity. Tom said afterwards that he was glad that we could show Rita that her old room and Danny's were being used by us rather than occupied by anyone else. Rita was amazed by the smallness of her former bedroom. She recognised quite a number of pieces of furniture and other things.

Rita told us that she was allowed less freedom than Danny, but was beginning to go out and be more independent. She had not kept up any of her old interests, like singing, dancing and swimming. She had clearly spent a lot of time looking after the small children in the extended family, and on cooking and housework. She was trying to watch less television. She volunteered her dislike of illegal drugs and said she did not smoke. She went to church twice on Sundays.

'Do you think much about the past, Rita?' I asked at one point, when a short silence threatened to grow longer.

'I do think about it sometimes.' We waited for her to say more.

'What do you remember best?' I prompted.

'Holidays,' she answered with a grin.

We began to talk about some of the holidays we had had together. Tom showed Rita the pictures of our holiday that summer. Rita had not had a family holiday since leaving us. She said that she had seen some pictures of herself and Danny as children, which we had sent to Cynthia years ago. Tom promised to compile an album of photos for each of them. Rita was pleased about that and told us how she enjoyed taking pictures with her camera and that Jackson had lots of cameras she could borrow. I wondered how much she saw him, but it gave us a clue for a birthday present.

We went on to talk about Rita's possessions, which were in the loft. I promised to bring them down for her next time, so she could decide what she wanted to have. She was surprised we had kept anything and liked the idea of seeing some of her old things, even though the clothes would be too small, the books and toys too childish.

Rita seemed not to have much money to spend on clothes. I asked about her hair, remembering the plaiting sessions.

'I put too many chemicals on it, trying to straighten it. I damaged it, but I'm growing the damaged hair out. I plait it at nights and brush it out in the day for the moment, but when it's grown out, then I'll have it short.'

'It was very brave of you to come and see us, Rita,' Tom said a little later. 'We felt nervous about it and I bet it made you feel the same.'

Rita heaved a sigh and then laughed with what seemed like relief. 'It did, but I thought the longer I leave it the harder it will get.'

'It must seem like a long time ago that you lived with us. Do you think things have turned out for the best?' I asked this question rather awkwardly. What I meant was that we would understand if Rita had no regrets about leaving.

'I suppose so.' Was it my imagination or did she seem sad?

'Do you sometimes wish your grandmother had brought you up from the beginning?' I said. Rita had been here for some time by then and no one had mentioned Mrs Graham. Our decision not to mention her unless Rita did had begun to seem too artificial.

'No,' Rita answered and laughed. 'Granny's so strict.' We all laughed at the way she said this. Her lips curled into a smile just as they used to when she was little.

'She's getting older now so she can't tell me what to do so much and she can't do so much herself,' said Rita. 'She likes to do the cooking and I do the washing up. I don't have the time to do the cooking so much any more.' I found myself able to ask after Mrs Graham. She was well in some ways, but had a number of health problems.

Then somehow we had said everything there was to say on a first visit. Rita rose to go and I looked at my watch. To my amazement, I saw that she had spent nearly three hours with us. Conversation had ebbed and flowed, but she had not run away after a short time as she could have done.

'We hope you will come and see us again soon, now we are in touch,' said Tom. 'Perhaps you would like to come and have a meal with us.'

Rita looked as pleased as Tom and I felt. She refused a lift, despite the fact that it was dark and raining, as she was not going straight home. Then she said goodbye and was gone. We waved and smiled from the doorstep and from under her umbrella she smiled too.

It had been an extraordinary afternoon for all of us and Tom and I felt it had gone better than expected. Two weeks later, we sent Rita a book about photography and some film for her seventeenth birthday. We added a card with an invitation to come and see us again soon. We had embarked on a new kind of relationship with Danny and Rita – one of their choosing. We could not tell what its future would be, but Tom and I were happy to know them as young adults and relieved that they had so far navigated the tricky waters of their lives with some success.

I retrieved Rita's portrait from the cellar and once again her face smiled out from the wall of the sitting room. We matched it with a photograph of Danny.

Epilogue in 2006

It is over twelve years since that afternoon with Rita. We have slowly developed the new relationship with Danny and Rita, which we feel is unforced on either side. They clearly belong to their birth family, but they have a connection with us. We have not seen the other members of the Graham family again.

We stayed for many years in the home we had shared with Danny and Rita, in a house where at first it was impossible not to think of them. We saw no reason to move at the time, nor did we intend to place ourselves beyond their reach, even though we accepted that the choice of whether to see us or not, at least at first, had to be largely theirs. When we moved, not far away, it was for other reasons.

We have longed to know Danny's and Rita's side of the story – how they felt about being adopted, about being black with white parents, what they think they may have gained from adoption, what it was like to go and live with their birth family, whether they have any regrets about anything. Danny is too immersed in the present to want to go over the past, but we have recently talked more with Rita about her childhood.

Danny is a confident, good-humoured, talkative and attractive young man. Since his first visit to us of his own free will at fifteen, we have seen him irregularly, every few months, although less so recently. He used to drop in without warning, when he was passing or when he felt like seeing us, but now telephones first and keeps in touch by phone when he is too busy to see us. We never tried to persuade Danny to return to us, as this was so obviously not what he wanted. At the age when most young people struggle to achieve some independence from their family, Danny, having known his birth family only from a distance, was keen to belong.

He continued to attend the same school. He left at the age of sixteen with some GCSEs. The continuity of his school life, and the freedom accorded him by his family, enabled him to keep up with his friends, both black and white. Always a hard worker, he took Saturday and holiday jobs in supermarkets or restaurants, sometimes near us, and friends of ours would often say they had seen him.

Danny became interested in the building trade through Jackson, and eventually got a degree in construction management. The course included short study tours abroad to look at construction methods, which he explained to us in great detail. He took photos and brought them to show us, neatly arranged in an album, echoing our photo albums of family events. While taking his degree, he found a part-time job with a construction company and is now working in his chosen field. He also works at weekends to supplement his income, and in addition belongs to the Territorial Army.

When he was twenty-two, Danny's grandmother sold her house and moved away. He was allocated a council flat where he still lives and which he has now bought, with a mortgage. He invited us once to a Sunday lunch, but generally prefers to come to us. He no longer attends church regularly.

Danny has had a number of girlfriends. He has a son of

eleven; his relationship with the mother ceased before their son was born. His son spends every weekend and many holidays with Danny, who draws on Rita extensively to help with child care. The boy will be starting secondary school this autumn. He is a gentle and charming child, who is growing in confidence. He has visited us many times, and we are very fond of him. He is clearly devoted to Danny, who now also has a baby daughter, from a different relationship. Danny sees his daughter as often as he can. He contributes financially to the upbringing of both his children.

Rita too stayed on at the same school, but left at sixteen without qualifications. Our impression is that the family expected her to do a great deal of cooking and child care, and put these responsibilities before her education. She took some courses after leaving school, however, and for some years worked for the NHS in an administrative post. Her life with the Grahams seemed from the start to be much more restricted than Danny's.

After her Saturday afternoon visit, we did not see her for over a year. She ignored a further invitation, and so we left it to her to decide. Eventually she contacted us and then, at the age of twenty, moved into her own flat, which made it easier for her to keep in touch.

Rita has a strong personality and a wonderful sense of humour. She has a little girl of three. All Rita's years of looking after small children in the family have made her an expert and confident mother. She has also developed a clear sense of purpose and ambitions. She is doing access courses to gain entrance to medical school.

She accepted family invitations to visit Jamaica several times, taking an interest in the history of Jamaica and her family's roots. She has also been to the United States and Canada to visit relatives.

She has a powerful singing voice. A few years ago, we arranged singing lessons for her and her teacher commended her voice. She has strong religious beliefs and is active in her local church community, where she sings as a soloist. She has made an attractive home of her flat and has invited us to visit, but, like Danny, she prefers to see us on our home ground.

Danny and Rita have both shown a measure of independence and self-sufficiency that has impressed us. They have faced many challenges with good humour and strength. They have not always seen eye to eye but, seventeen years after they left us, they are still in close contact with each other. They often talk on the phone and Rita sometimes cooks meals for Danny. She knows him well and is not afraid to give him advice. She is also an important person in the life of Danny's son, whom she often looks after at weekends and during holidays.

Sadly, Jackson was killed in a car crash while working in the United States a few years ago. Cynthia has kept in touch with us, the only relative of Danny and Rita to do so. Until recently, when her illness worsened, she wrote to us every Christmas and even on Mother's Day, and has sometimes sent birthday cards and presents. We always write back. Since Mr Graham died a few years ago, Mrs Graham divides her time between living in Jamaica with her sister, and living in England, so she can see her adult children and grandchildren.

Reflections

I should like to finish with some reflections on our experience as adoptive parents. This offers an opportunity to feel more in touch with the reader, who may well be involved in fostering or adoption, or contemplating it, or may be working, directly or indirectly, with children who are fostered or adopted.

If this book had been published in the 1980s, when I wrote a first version, it would have been the story of a successful adoption. Some years later, it would have been about what is called a disrupted adoption. Instead, thirty years have passed since Tom and I first began to think about adopting and, as a result, the book chronicles an adoption, a disruption and a continuing relationship with Danny and Rita as young adults belonging to their birth family. I hope it is more useful now that I can take such a long view. However, as I started writing not long after Rita came to live with us, it is not entirely a view from a distance.

All the incidents really happened and all the dialogue reports conversations that took place at the time. The perspective is mine, although I have incorporated comments from Tom and Rita.

Our story begins a generation ago, in the 1970s, and some aspects of adoption have changed since then, but it also deals with themes which are highly relevant today. The main change is that transracial placements are now largely limited to intercountry adoptions. However, the adjustment of children to a new family, how they deal with loss and make new attachments and how they overcome, or adjust to, earlier adversity are matters which are timeless and these are also important themes in the book. In their early years with us, it was Danny's and Rita's attachments to people other than relatives which were important to them, in Rita's case to the Clark family and in Danny's case to Marion. It was Danny's and Rita's distress on being required to change their emotional attachments which was the main issue for us at first. Their ethnic background and family relationships were issues that by and large emerged later, as their consciousness of their circumstances grew.

Transracial adoption

When Tom and I, who are white, were applying to adopt, transracial adoption was an established practice. It would have been unthinkable for us to insist on taking a child of our own ethnic origin because, according to the views of the time, this would have been racist. However, by 1981, two years after Rita came to live with us, and only a year after Danny joined us, the climate of opinion had changed in favour of ethnic matching. We support this approach because it must be in the interests of the child to have as much in common with the adoptive family as possible. However, there may be occasions where transracial adoption is indicated, for example, if a family of the same ethnicity cannot be found within a reasonable period of time, for whatever reason. This would involve a commitment from the adopters to promote a positive ethnic identity in the child, as far as they are able to do so.

The social workers at the time stressed, and we understood, the importance of a positive commitment to the child's culture of origin. Living in a largely, but not entirely, white community, we did our best – hence our attempts to get to know black families, the plaiting sessions, the hunt for black dolls, the search for books containing pictures of black children. We knew that in no substantial sense could we possibly provide Danny and Rita with experience of their culture, and this was one reason why we had encouraged the relationship with Jackson's family. Cynthia's family was never really accessible to us as her illness prevented her from providing the necessary pathway. We saw Jackson's family as offering Danny and Rita an experience of black culture in Britain. We knew there were risks, although I do not think we fully appreciated what might happen, but we also thought that it was important for them to know their other family and that family's culture.

This raises the question of exactly what their birth family's culture is and whether it is what Danny and Rita want. Mrs Graham's culture is based on her Jamaican background, her experiences of coming as an immigrant to Britain, and her life here. Danny's and Rita's culture is that of young black people who were born here. They had to sort out their own identity, not as small children, but in early adolescence – a huge task for them. Rita says that it was not until she went to secondary school, where there were many more black children than at her primary school, that she fully realised what an unusual position she was in. She did not have any experience of the kind of life that other black pupils in her school were leading; their language, references and jokes were at first a mystery to her.

Our view is that Danny's and Rita's years with us were not wasted – they are at ease with white people in a way they may not otherwise have been. The Graham family has never wavered from the view that Danny and Rita should have been placed with them from the beginning. They do not want to hear about Danny's and Rita's life with us and do not give any credit to it, so Danny and Rita can only look back and judge our shared past by talking to us or to friends. This book has given us an additional reason for discussing our shared past with Rita. Danny has chosen not to participate.

Reuniting siblings

For Danny and Rita, it was more a question of uniting than reuniting them as they were parted when Rita was only two months old. Whilst we were persuaded of the need to bring them together, the story shows there were undoubtedly difficulties as a result. Social work guidance says that siblings should be placed together if possible, but whether or not it is a good idea in any one case will depend on the circumstances.

Open adoption

Open adoption carries risks, but is increasingly the practice now that most children are no longer babies when they are adopted. However, keeping in touch by exchanging letters and cards (known as letterbox contact) is more common than face-to-face meetings. We were so bound to Danny and Rita in their childhood that we did not foresee their leaving us so young and so suddenly. It is shocking for a child of twelve to leave home. Yet their leaving was probably inevitable, given our commitment to openness, the proximity and nature of their grandmother, and the lack of professional support and guidance. In the long run, it was for the best in terms of their sense of belonging to their birth family and to black British culture. The main disadvantages for them are that their education suffered and they are financially poorer. Danny has made up for loss of education and Rita is doing so, but it is always harder later on.

Danny's and Rita's leaving us caused deep distress, but there is compensation in the fact that we now have a good relationship with them. That relationship, and our relationship with their children, is hard to describe. There is no ready vocabulary for it. We are no longer mum and dad and we are not seen by their children as grandparents. Danny has sometimes referred to us as his white parents. There are parental overtones in our relationship, and we are reliable older figures for Danny's son and Rita's daughter. We shared eleven years of living with Danny and Rita and more years of knowing each other subsequently. Their lives are of enormous interest and concern to us and we hope we will continue to know them well. This matters more to us than trying to label the relationship.

One feature of open adoption that was new to us was the prominent role played by the grandmother, Mrs Graham. We only knew of Jackson's mother after Rita came to live with us. Rita's family was presented to us almost entirely in terms of Cynthia and Jackson and there was no mention of any claim by Mrs Graham in respect of the children until Danny entered our lives. Because our own mothers had less central roles in the extended family, we were unprepared for how much power Mrs Graham wielded. She is a true matriarch.

Understanding children

There should be greater preparation for adoption and more time should be given to family placement work on social work courses. Our social workers gave us the best help and guidance that they could at the time. But they may not have had the benefit of sufficient experience, expertise or resources to support us in dealing with Danny and Rita and their birth family. We spent a lot of time puzzling over the children's behaviour, particularly Danny's, in an attempt to understand it. We tried to be consistent, we were always concerned and involved, and we tried to offer Danny ways of dealing with the world when he was in difficulties. Fortunately, research evidence is growing about the needs and behaviour of children who are fostered or adopted, particularly about the many questions of contact with birth families and pattern of recovery from earlier adversity. Those dealing with children who need new families will benefit from the greater knowledge at their disposal.

Conclusion

We adopted Danny and Rita in the context of policy at the time and we are fully aware that these days, children in similar circumstances would be likely to be placed, if possible, with their birth family. We can only say that we hope Danny and Rita have benefited from their years with us. Knowing them has enriched our lives enormously. Their departure from our home and family was not the end of the adoption, but a chapter in a continuing story. Despite the tensions and problems of the past, we are glad of the friendly and positive relationship we have with them now. We look forward to a future that will continue to include Danny and Rita and their families.

ALSO AVAILABLE

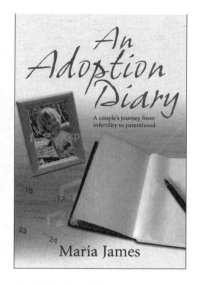

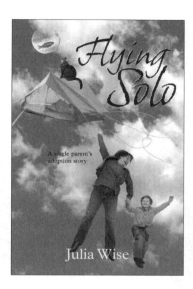

An Adoption Diary

This is a true story of an adoption – a story that follows Maria's and Rob's adoption of a two-year-old child. Spanning almost four years, this enthralling diary chronicles the highs and lows along the way, until the approved adopters become parents for the very first time.

This is an inspirational story of one couple's emotional journey to become a family, which gives a fascinating insight into adoption in Britain today.

Flying Solo

This book tells Julia's story of adopting a child on her own. In this heart-warming and humorous account, Julia lays bare her mistakes and misconceptions and shares with the reader some practical advice and some top tips. A must-read for potential single adopters.

Available from BAAF Publications
Saffron House
6–10 Kirby Street
London EC1N 8TS
Tel: 020 7421 2604
Email: pubs.sales@baaf.org.uk

www.baaf.org.uk

£7.95

Interested in adoption?

Then visit www.bemyparent.org.uk

- View the profiles of children in the UK needing an adoptive or permanent foster family
- Multimedia content, including video and audio
- Make enquiries directly to the agency online
- Comprehensive information on adoption and fostering
- Access 24/7
- Safe and secure website

Live from Spring 2007

A BAAF service,
BAAF, Saffron House,
6 – 10 Kirby Street,
London EC1N 8TS.

Registered charity 275689